DEE YATES

Write Your Own Damn Story

Building an empire without asking for permission.

DEE YATES
California

*For the girl who failed English and was told she'd never make it.
For my son Rowdy, who proves every day that different is a
blessing.
For Ronnie, my rock in every storm.
For my mother Vickie, who taught me what unconditional love
looks like.
For my father Donald, who taught me to ball up my fist and never
back down.
For the women who build legacies without permission.
And for everyone who was told they weren't enough—
this is your permission to prove them wrong.*

"Stop waiting for someone to tell you you're ready. Stop asking for the permission that's never coming. Stop playing small to make others comfortable. Your story is waiting. Write it."

-DEE YATES

Contents

Prologue

Prologue

Nobody gave me permission to build this life. Nobody handed me a roadmap or a mentor or a trust fund. Nobody said "Here's how you go from failing English to owning a 58-year-old legacy publication." I figured it out. Made mistakes. Lost everything. Rebuilt. And kept going.

And here's what I know about you right now: You didn't pick up this book by accident. Something brought you here. Maybe it's exhaustion from waiting for permission that's never coming. Maybe it's a rage from being told you're not qualified. Maybe it's that vision burning inside you that everyone else says is impossible. Maybe you're just done. Done asking, done waiting, done playing small to make other people comfortable.

Good. That's exactly where transformation starts.

This book is the foundation of my keynote, the message I deliver on stages about building legacies without asking for permission. About creating opportunities instead of waiting for them. About doing the work nobody else is willing to do until you become undeniable. This isn't motivational fluff for people who need their hands held. This is for fighters.

Builders. People willing to stand on their own two feet and make things happen when everyone else is making excuses.

Let me tell you how this book came to be.

I was asked to speak at the Cowgirl Collective in Cartersville, Georgia. When I got that invitation, I was overwhelmed with honor because I have so much to say. For the last year, I had files on my computer full of inspirational ideas and pieces of my story. I had been transcribing things constantly on my phone, journaling in my notes app, capturing the ideas and thoughts and principles that helped me achieve what I've done. How I've kept my mind and my emotions and my life in balance and harmony. The real key points.

So I created a mastery list. A principles list. I developed an outline for the talk. It was only supposed to be 30 minutes, so I paired it down into condensed ideas and key points. I got really good at organizing my thoughts.

And that outline ended up becoming chapters. It became the bones of this book. I took all of my transcriptions, all of my notes, all of my ideas, and I developed it into what you're holding right now.

I used technology to help me write it. AI became my editor. And it has become one of the most important tools I've ever had. Don't let anybody ever downplay the use of technology as tools. It's the reason this book is completed today.

So let me ask you something that matters: What are you

building that the world keeps telling you isn't possible? What vision keeps you awake at night? What door has been slammed in your face so many times you've started to believe maybe they're right, maybe you don't belong?

I need you to understand: That door, That's not the only door. And the people who slammed it, They don't get to decide your story. You do.

Let me be clear about what you're holding: This book isn't perfect. You'll find grammatical errors. Sentence fragments. Run-ons. Probably typos I missed. I failed English multiple times. But here's what I know: Having something to say is more important than perfect grammar. I'd rather get paint on the canvas, messy and imperfect, than wait for perfection and never start. This isn't about grammatical flex. This is about grit and determination in your business and your life. This is about proving you can have it all if you're willing to do what others won't.

So if you're the type who'll put this book down over a comma splice, go ahead. This isn't for you. But if you value raw truth over polished bullshit, if you care more about results than credentials, if you're ready to build something that matters even when the world says you don't belong, you're exactly where you need to be.

As someone who failed English multiple times and went on to publish books and own a successful women's magazine and a 58-year-old legacy publication, as someone who lost everything and rebuilt multiple businesses, as someone who was told I'd never make money with a camera and documented thousands of women across decades, I'm on a mission to help people just like you stop waiting for permission and start building the empire you were meant to create.

Because I've watched too many brilliant people die with their dreams still inside them. Too many visionaries sitting on the sidelines waiting for someone to say "you're ready." Too many fighters who gave up because they didn't have the right credentials or the right connections or the right last name. And I refuse to let that be your story.

Here's what I built: A 25-year photography career documenting thousands of women. Multiple businesses. Books preserving Western culture. Owner and publisher of a successful women's magazine. Ownership of Ropers Sports News, a publication that's been the bible of team roping since 1968. A platform teaching others how to do the same. And I did it without asking permission. Without waiting for the "right time." Without credentials that said I was qualified… And I am just getting started.

I made my own opportunities. Created my own doors. Built my own tables when I wasn't invited to theirs.

And you can too.

Building without permission doesn't mean building without a plan. It doesn't mean throwing spaghetti at the wall and hoping something sticks. It means understanding the real game, the one they don't teach in business school because they don't want people like us to know the rules.

This book shows you exactly how. Not theory. Not motivational quotes. Real stories. Real strategies. Real lessons from someone who's actually done it. Someone who lost everything and rebuilt stronger. Someone who bought businesses without business degrees. Someone who walked into old boys' clubs and <u>made</u> them make space.

You're going to learn: How to build when you have no credentials and nobody believes in you. How to handle obstacles and turn them into opportunities. How to create your own doors when all the others are closed. How to build multiple income streams that actually work. How to preserve what you love while making money doing it. How to become so undeniable they have no choice but to pay attention.

This is the exact process I used to: Build a photography business that generated consistent income without formal training. Run a successful women's magazine. Take over a dying 58-year-old publication and transform it into a thriving legacy brand. Publish books that preserve culture and create lasting impact. Rebuild after losing everything and come back stronger. Walk into rooms where I wasn't wanted and prove I belonged through work, not words.

And here's my promise to you: If you're willing to do the work, if you're willing to get uncomfortable, if you're willing to stop making excuses and start making moves, this book will show you exactly how to build the life you want instead of accepting the life you were given.

Here's what I need from you: Stop waiting. Stop making excuses about why now isn't the right time. Stop letting other people's limitations become your ceiling. The right time is now. The permission you need is already yours. And the only person who has to believe in your vision first is you.

The truth is, nobody wants to say it out loud: In five years, you'll either be living the life you're building right now, or you'll be explaining why you didn't. You'll either be owning your empire, or you'll be working in someone else's. You'll either be the person who took the risk, or the person who played it safe and has regrets. There's no neutral position.

And I know which one you're going to choose. Because you're still here. You didn't put this book down when I warned you about the grammar. You're reading this right now because something inside you knows: This is your time. Your turn. Your moment to stop asking and start building.

So let me tell you who this book is actually for: This is for the kid who failed classes but has bigger dreams than anyone who passed. This is for the person rebuilding after losing everything. This is for the fighter walking into rooms where they're not wanted. This is for the visionary sitting on a project everyone says is impossible. This is for the builder who's tired of waiting for permission from people who'll never give it. This is for you.

And here's what this book is not: This isn't a blueprint to copy my exact path. This isn't a promise that it'll be easy. This isn't permission to skip the hard work. This is the truth about what it actually takes to build something from nothing. To walk through fire and come out stronger. To lose everything and rebuild bigger. To prove everyone wrong not with words, but with work.

This is about writing your own damn story. Not waiting for someone to write it for you. Not letting "no" be the final answer. Not accepting limitations other people try to put on you. You want something? Figure out how to build it. Don't know how? Learn. Can't find a mentor? Teach yourself. Nobody will hire you? Hire yourself. Doors closed? Build your own.

That's the message. That's what I m offering. That's what this book delivers. No victim mentality. No excuses. No waiting for perfect conditions. Just relentless forward motion until you become impossible to ignore.

One more thing before we start: I'm not going to hold your hand through this. I'm not going to tell you it's all going to be okay. I'm not going to give you participation trophies for showing up. Because the world doesn't work that way. The world rewards people who do hard things when everyone else makes excuses. The world makes space for people who refuse to quit. The world bends to people who are so committed to their vision that "no" becomes irrelevant.

That's who I'm writing this for. That's who you're about to become.

You ready?

Let's go build something they can't ignore. Your empire starts on the next page. No more permission. No more waiting. No more excuses. Just you and the work.

Let's go.

1

California Girl

I grew up in Lockeford, California—a town so small you've never heard of it, and that's exactly the point. Central Valley. Vineyards and orchards as far as you could see. Gravel roads that turned your bike tires white with dust. Summers spent barefoot, coming home only when the streetlights buzzed on—except we didn't have streetlights, so you came home when the sky turned pink and your stomach started growling.

We were poor, but I didn't know it. That's the thing about poverty when you're a kid—if everyone around you lives the same way, you think it's normal. Clothes with holes weren't embarrassing, they were just clothes. Vegetables from the garden weren't "farm-to-table"—they were dinner. We didn't have a lot, but we had land under our feet and faith in our hearts and chores that needed doing.

My family's story is a story of survival. On my father's side:

German immigrants from North Dakota who nearly froze to death their first winter in America. They dug holes in the ground just to survive. Literal holes. When spring came, they kept moving west until they hit California's Central Valley, where the dirt was rich and the winters didn't kill you. Six generations of struggle followed them—farm laborers, poverty, alcoholism passed down like a cursed heirloom.

On my mother's side: fifteen generations in America, stretching back to the late 1400s. Her people founded Hunt, Texas. My grandfather, Dan Lock, was Roy Rogers' ranch manager and trained his horses—including Trigger himself. Dale Evans was my mother's godmother. There's a photograph somewhere of Dale holding my mother as a baby, and sometimes I think about that picture and wonder how a family can travel so far from Hollywood's golden age to a farmhouse in Lockeford where the toilet didn't always work.

But here's what I understand now that I didn't then: my grandfather wasn't just working with horses. He was part of the early era of media —Roy Rogers and Dale Evans weren't just cowboys, they were publishers, filmmakers, storytellers who shaped how America saw the West. That legacy—that understanding that the story matters was embraced way before me.

Here's what I inherited: not money. Not a business. Not connections or a trust fund or a leg up. I inherited work ethic. I inherited pride. I inherited responsibility. And somewhere, buried deep, I inherited an understanding that documenting the West—preserving its stories, its culture, its people—was sacred work.

I want to be careful here, because my father is gone now—he passed in August 2025, just under a year before I'm writing this—and he deserves his dignity and honor. But you can't tell a true story by leaving out the hard parts, and my father's drinking was the hardest part of my childhood.

There was a version of my dad that was wonderful—hardworking, proud, funny in that dry way that catches you off guard. And there was a version of my dad that emerged when the bottle came out, and that version was unpredictable, sometimes scary, often absent even when he was sitting right there in the room.

I watched my mother navigate it. I watched the way she held everything together with her bare hands while the ground shifted beneath her. I watched the tension that lived in our house like an uninvited guest who wouldn't leave. And somewhere in there—somewhere between the good days and the bad days, between the hoping it would get better and the accepting that it probably wouldn't—I made a decision.

I decided I would never be a victim.

Not of circumstances. Not of other people's choices. Not of the poverty or the chaos or the pain that I was born into. I didn't choose where I started, but I would damn sure choose where I ended up.

I didn't have the words for it then. I was just a kid with

dirty knees and hand-me-down shirts, watching my mother hold everything together while my father's drinking pulled everything apart. But something crystallized in me during those years, something hard and certain and unbreakable. This is not going to be my story. This pattern stops with me.

I would not be abused. I would not stay poor. I would not let the chaos around me become the chaos inside me. I would not accept that because my father's side of the family had struggled for generations, and I was destined to do the same. I rejected that inheritance completely.

I would fight. I would work. I would build something different. I would break the cycle or die trying.

This wasn't some noble declaration I made standing on a mountaintop. This was survival instinct. This was a scared kid looking at her family's pattern and saying not me, never me. I will never be the person who gives up. I will never be the person who lets life happen to them. I will never be the person who plays victim to their circumstances.

That decision—that silent, fierce, stubborn refusal to accept the hand I'd been dealt—would become the foundation of everything I would build. It would carry me through losing everything in the 2008 crash. It would carry me through depression so deep I couldn't get off the couch. It would carry me through being told I didn't belong, that I wasn't good enough, that girls like me don't build empires. That decision, made when I was too young to understand its full weight, would save my life over and over again.

The truth: you can't build an empire if you're playing victim to your story. You can't create anything lasting if you're waiting for someone to save you. You can't break generational patterns if you're still blaming your ancestors for passing them down.

At some point, you have to stand up and say: this is my life now. These are my choices. This is my responsibility. Nobody's coming to fix this for me, so I better figure it out myself.

That's what I decided, standing in a farmhouse in Lockeford at maybe nine or ten years old. I didn't know it would shape everything. I just knew I wasn't going to drown.

If childhood teaches you about your family's place in the world, high school teaches you about your own. And what I learned was brutal: there was a social ladder, and I didn't see myself on it. I could see it so clearly—who mattered and who didn't, who wore the right clothes and who wore whatever their older sister had outgrown. I watched the popular kids move through the hallways like they owned them, and I watched myself slip into the background.

I wasn't one of them. I knew it in my bones. They were nice to me, but only because I kept showing up. So I found my people: the ag kids, the ones who didn't fit in the shiny boxes either. We were the ones with calluses and early mornings, the ones who knew how to work because we'd been working since we were old enough to carry a bucket.

Academically, I was average. Bored, mostly. History class felt like someone reading me a phone book—names and dates that didn't connect to anything real. Math was fine. Science was fine. Everything was fine.

Except English.

I failed English. Not once. Multiple times.

I want you to understand what that felt like—sitting in a classroom, staring at an essay prompt, knowing that the words in my head would come out wrong on the page. Knowing that everyone else seemed to have some secret code I'd never been given. The red marks on my papers. The disappointed looks. The growing certainty that I was fundamentally broken in some essential way.

You're not smart enough. You'll never be a writer. People like you don't get to tell stories—you get to listen to other people tell theirs. That was The Voice. I didn't have a name for it then, but it was there, whispering in the back of my mind every time I picked up a pen. Telling me I was too poor, too uneducated, too country, too wrong to ever amount to anything.

The Voice is a perception of self and should not have much ground in your formal opinion of yourself. But I didn't know that yet. What I knew was shame. Deep, burning, secret shame that I carried like a stone in my pocket. The girl who failed English. The girl who couldn't put sentences together. The girl who had something to say but no way to say it. I buried that shame so deep I thought no one could see it. But it was there, shaping everything I did, every dream I was too afraid to dream.

Who do you think you are? That was The Voice's favorite question. Who do you think you are, young lady?

And then, junior year, I took a photography class. I don't remember why. Maybe I needed an elective. Maybe something drew me there without my understanding. But I walked into Mr. Thielen's classroom, and for the first time in my academic life, something clicked.

Behind the camera, I wasn't the girl who failed English. Behind the camera, I was an A-plus student. The difference was physical—I could feel it. When I held that camera, my hands were steady. When I looked through the viewfinder, the world made sense in a way it never had on a page. I wasn't trying to translate the pictures in my head into words. I was just making the pictures. Direct. Immediate. True.

I checked out a film camera from the high school when I was sixteen. I still remember the weight of it in my hands, the mechanical click of the shutter, the magic of watching an image emerge in the darkroom. Light becoming memory. Moment becoming permanent. This. This was what I was supposed to do.

I didn't fail at this. I excelled. And something shifted. Not everything—The Voice was still there, still whispering—but something fundamental changed. For the first time, I had evidence that I wasn't broken. I just came with different instructions.

When I was eighteen, I stood in my mother's kitchen and

said something that sounded crazy even as it came out of my mouth: "Someday I'm going to own my own magazine."

My mother didn't laugh. She didn't tell me to be realistic, to set my sights lower, to remember that girls like us didn't do things like that. She just looked at me—this woman who had held our family together through impossible years—and I think she saw something in my eyes. Maybe she saw the same stubborn refusal that had kept her going. Maybe she saw the photography, the way I lit up behind the camera. Maybe she just believed in me when I couldn't quite believe in myself.

She didn't say, "That's impossible." She didn't say, "Who do you think you are?"

She let me say it out loud, and that was enough.

I was thinking about fashion magazines. Vogue. Elle. The glossy pages filled with beautiful women and stunning photography. I'd spent my teenage years flipping through those magazines, studying the light, the poses, the way a single image could tell a story. I wanted to create that—portraits, fashion, beauty. I wanted to make women feel seen and celebrated through my lens.

I had no idea that years later, my path would twist back to my Western roots. That I'd end up documenting cowgirls instead of models, preserving rodeo culture instead of chasing fashion trends. That the magazine I'd eventually own wouldn't be glossy fashion at all—it would be a 58-year-old Western sports publication that I'd transform from a newspaper format into the magazine I'd always dreamed of creating.

But at eighteen, standing in my mother's kitchen, I just wanted to photograph beautiful women and put them in a magazine.

I couldn't know, standing in that kitchen at eighteen, that it would take me almost sixteen years to make that declaration true. I couldn't know about the photography business I would build, the ranch I would help build and have foreclosed, the magazine I would acquire and sell, the second magazine I would save from extinction. I couldn't know that in 2007, I'd marry a man named Ronnie who would become my rock through all of it—the losses, the rebuilds, the impossible days when I wanted to quit. I couldn't know about the 2008 crash that would leave me standing in an empty house with a baby on my hip. I couldn't know about the Hospital advertiser who would demand my silence, or the phone call where a man would ask me "Who do you think you are, young lady?" or the moment I would find my voice deep and sharp enough to answer him. I couldn't know about the cowgirl book that would take eight years to finish, or the day I would forgive my father for everything.

All I knew, standing in that kitchen, was that I had something to say. And even if my grammar was terrible, even if I couldn't pass an English class, even if The Voice told me every day that I wasn't enough—I was going to find a way to say it.

* * *

[THE LESSON]: You Are Not Broken

You are not broken. You come with instructions.

Every challenge, every wound, every struggle has been teaching you what you need to become who you are. I failed English, and that failure pushed me toward photography— toward telling stories with images instead of words. I grew up poor, and that poverty taught me to work for everything I wanted. I had a father who drank, and that pain taught me to build a life where I would never be a victim.

Your job is not to fix yourself. Your job is to understand yourself. The things you think are your weaknesses? They're instructions. They're pointing you toward what you need, what you're capable of, who you're meant to become.

My inability to write a grammatically perfect sentence pushed me toward photography. And that skill led me to magazines. And magazines led me to publishing. And publishing led me here, to this book, writing imperfect sentences that I pray will change your life.

The Voice told me I was broken. The Voice was wrong. Self-value is the ultimate boundary. When you understand that you are not broken—that you simply come with different instructions—you stop trying to fit into boxes designed for someone else. You stop apologizing for being different. You stop waiting for permission to be yourself. You start building from where you are, with what you have, exactly as you are.

[YOUR TURN]

Write down three things about yourself that you've labeled as "broken" or "wrong." Maybe it's something you failed at. Maybe it's a part of your past you're ashamed of. Maybe it's a way you're different from everyone else. Be honest. Write it down.

____

____

____

____

____

____

Now, beside each one, reframe it as an instruction. What does this trait teach you about your needs? Your boundaries? Your desires? How might this "flaw" actually be guiding you toward growth? For me, "I failed English" became "I'm a visual storyteller who needs to work with images." What does your failure become when you reframe it?

____

____

____

____

____

____

Finally, answer this question: Where did you start? What was your ordinary world? Not the story you tell at cocktail parties. The real one. The gravel roads and hand-me-down clothes and kitchen-table dreams that nobody but you remembers.

____

____

____

____

____

____

That's not your limitation. That's your foundation.

Your circumstances don't get the final say. Your decisions do.

2

Costco Camera

Nobody tells you that chasing dreams looks nothing like you think it will.

In the movies, there's a montage. Inspirational music swells. The hero gets a scholarship or a lucky break or a wise mentor who hands them the keys to the kingdom. Everything unfolds like it was meant to be.

In real life, you stand in Costco with your parents, staring at a camera that costs $600, which might as well be $6 million when you're eighteen and broke, and you think: This is it. This is where it starts.

My parents bought me that camera. Let me be clear about what that meant. We weren't a family that had $600 lying around for dreams. We were a family that had $600 lying around for emergencies, maybe, if we'd been saving. This wasn't a casual purchase. This was a sacrifice.

My father had strong opinions about that camera purchase. He always had opinions about my decisions, and he wasn't shy about voicing them. "Photographers are a dime a dozen," he'd told me more than once. He wanted to make sure I understood the value of what they were giving me, that this wasn't just a toy but a tool I'd need to master. He wanted me to have a "real job," something stable, something predictable. But despite his doubts about whether photography could ever be a legitimate career, he and my mother stood in that Costco aisle with me anyway.

"If we're investing in this," he told me, "you're going to pay us back. Twenty-five dollars every month until it's paid off. You want to be a photographer? Then you learn what it means to earn your equipment."

That was my father, always teaching, always making sure I understood that nothing worthwhile came easy. He made a little receipt book, handwritten, where I'd record each payment. It wasn't about the money. It was about the lesson. About understanding that dreams have a price, and you pay that price yourself.

So I made $25 payments back to them. Every month, until it was paid off. That camera wasn't a gift; it was a loan. An investment. A statement that said: If you want something, you earn it. That was my first lesson in equal exchange. That was the first time I understood that value isn't given, it's created through the exchange of effort, commitment, and follow-through.

The Voice had opinions, of course. You think a camera makes you a photographer? You think buying equipment makes you legitimate? Real photographers go to art school. Real photographers have connections. Real photographers don't come from Lockeford.

I didn't have an answer for The Voice. I just had a camera and a hunger that wouldn't quit.

For graduation, my parents gave me a portrait lens. Another sacrifice. Another statement of belief in something I hadn't yet proven.

My father might have doubted that photography could be a real career, but he and my mother bought me that lens anyway. Despite his concerns about whether I could make a living taking pictures, he believed in teaching me to work for what I wanted. Maybe he recognized that same stubborn refusal to quit that he'd instilled in me. Maybe they both just loved me enough to bet on me.

Either way, I had my tools. Now I needed to learn how to use them.

My first gig was a wedding, and I did it for free. I want you to understand that. I didn't charge a dime. I showed up with my Costco camera and my portrait lens and my absolutely unearned confidence, and I photographed someone's entire wedding, one of the most important days of their life, for nothing.

I had no portfolio. No experience. No proof that I could do what I said I could do. All I had was the willingness to start ugly.

I developed all the film myself. Stood in the darkroom watching images emerge from the chemical bath, praying I hadn't screwed up the most important moments. The first kiss. The father-daughter dance. The rings. I gave them four-by-six copies of everything I photographed, and I held my breath waiting to see if they were any good.

I hadn't screwed them up. The photos were good. Not perfect, I had so much to learn, but good. Good enough that when I looked at them, I thought: I can do this. I can actually do this. All my photos were decent right off the bat because I had been studying in high school for a couple years before I got going. I had built up enough confidence and did it anyway.

The Voice was quieter that day. Not silent, but quieter.

My first paid wedding was $300. A trailer park in Northern California. A friend of my aunt's. Not exactly the glamorous start I'd dreamed about when I stood in that kitchen declaring I'd own a magazine someday. The client paid me $300 and gave me a big bag of film to shoot with.

But here's what that $300 taught me: someone believed my work was worth paying for. Not a lot. Not enough to live on. But something. And something is how every empire starts.

I took that $300 and I reinvested it. More film. More

developing supplies. Gas money to get to the next job. I wasn't building a business yet; I was building proof. Proof that I could do this. Proof that people would pay me. Proof that The Voice was wrong.

The trailer park bride got her photos, and they were beautiful. Her joy was just as real as any bride's in a cathedral. Her love was just as worthy of being preserved. I learned something that day that would serve me for the rest of my career: every story is worth telling well. It doesn't matter if it's a $300 wedding or a $10,000 wedding. When someone trusts you with their memories, you honor that trust completely.

Around this time, I did something that scared me, but I knew I had to do it anyway. There was a photographer in town, the best photographer in town, who did hand-tinted black and white portraits. Her work was exquisite. The kind of work that made you stop and stare, that made you feel something you couldn't name. She was everything I wanted to be.

She was beautiful and blonde and charismatic, and she was building her own business and was very successful. Extremely successful. Her portraits at the time, this was in the late 90s, were going for two, three, four, five thousand dollars apiece. And she was booked all year long. Clients flew from all over the country just to work with her.

Her studio was beautiful. Professional lighting. Elegant backdrops. Finished portraits displayed on the walls that looked like fine art. She had all these beautiful outfits and props and hat boxes and suitcases and little wagons and fake floral arrangements. She had mastered a technique that was dying out, hand-tinting black and white photographs with oils, bringing subtle color to skin tones and details while keeping the timeless quality of black and white. Each portrait took hours of meticulous work, and the results were stunning. This wasn't just photography. This was art.

When I happened to go to the best photographer in the area, I knew she was the best. And I knew I only wanted to learn from the best at a very young age. With all the fear in my guts, I walked up to her door, knocked on the door, and told her that I wanted to work for her.

I was eighteen years old, standing on this woman's porch with my heart pounding so hard I could hear it, holding a portfolio of about twelve images that I had matted myself. And I asked her: "Can I work for you? For free?"

She said yes. I still don't know why. Maybe she saw something in me. Maybe she just needed free help. But she let me into her world, and for that summer, I absorbed everything I could.

She took me all around and showed me everything. She took me down to the basement of this old house in the downtown of where I grew up, and down there she had all of her printing equipment. She was hand printing in a darkroom, all of her photos. Then she showed me the kitchen of that house, which was all set up just for hand painting, and she taught me how to hand paint these photos.

Hand-tinting and Darkroom techniques. How to handle

clients, how to make them feel seen, how to draw out their best selves in front of the camera. How to pose subjects, how to work with natural light, how to create that perfect soft focus that made her portraits look painterly. She taught me things you can't learn from a college course or a book. She taught me the craft. How to command her price. How to be a well paid artist. Eventually she let me go on some photo shoots with her, and I started learning how to handle clients and how to pose children and family members in these photos.

I was so in love with everything that she did.

I worked for free, and I would have paid her for the education I received. This is what I mean when I say relationships are currency. I had no money to offer. I had no connections, no credentials, no fancy degree. What I had was time, willingness, and hunger. I traded those things for knowledge, and that knowledge was worth more than any paycheck.

And then it went wrong.

I'd been developing my own style. Taking what I learned and making it my own, which is what every student eventually does, if they're any good. I started selling some of my work at a local street fair. Hand-tinted portraits, the techniques I'd learned, filtered through my own eye. I had about ten of my own 8x10 colored prints, photos of little kids at the beach and little kids fishing and little kids smelling flowers. I was in someone else's booth, selling the matted prints for about $25 each.

Her husband saw me there.

His voice cut through the crowd: "You STOLE her techniques! You're a THIEF!"

Everyone turned to look. I was eighteen years old, standing behind my booth with hand-tinted portraits I'd created with my own hands, and this grown man was screaming at me like I'd committed a crime.

People were staring. Some stopped to watch. I felt my face burning, my hands shaking. I wanted to disappear. I wanted the ground to open up and swallow me whole.

He was livid. He called his wife, obviously controlling her business, told her that she was to never see me again or let me in the studio again. And then he called me and berated me and told me I had no business learning his wife's talents and techniques and then using them on my own.

I tried to explain, that I'd learned from his wife, that she'd taught me willingly, that I'd created my own work. But he kept yelling. Kept accusing. Kept making a scene until I finally packed up my booth and left.

I went home that night and told my father what happened. He listened to the whole story, his jaw tight, and when I finished he said, "You didn't steal a damn thing. You learned from someone who was willing to teach you, then you created your own work. That's exactly how it's supposed to work. Ignore him and move on."

But even with his reassurance, I thought about quitting. I really did. I thought about how much easier it would be to stop. To accept that The Voice was right, that people like me don't get to do things like this, that I was foolish for ever thinking I could build something from nothing.

The Voice had a field day. See? You don't belong in this world. You're a fraud. You took something that wasn't yours, and now everyone knows it. You should quit. You should go back to Lockeford and get a real job and stop pretending you're something you're not.

That night, I didn't quit. I woke up the next morning, and I picked up my camera, and I kept going. Not because I had some grand realization. Not because I suddenly believed in myself. But because the alternative, giving up, felt worse than the shame of that street fair. Worse than The Voice. Worse than anything.

I had tasted what it felt like to create something. To capture a moment and make it permanent. To hand someone a photograph and watch their face change when they saw themselves through my eyes. It was through those moments that I saw I had value to others. I wasn't willing to give that up. Not for a screaming man. Not for The Voice. Not for anyone.

Here's what I know now that I didn't know then: every mentor relationship has a shelf life. Some mentors teach you what to do. Some mentors teach you what not to do. Some mentors become lifelong friends, and some mentors become cautionary tales. You can learn from all of them.

That photographer taught me technique. Her husband taught me something else entirely, he taught me that some people will resent your growth. That taking what you've learned and making it your own isn't theft; it's the whole point. That the people who scream at you for succeeding are usually the people who are afraid of being surpassed.

I didn't steal anything. I learned. And then I created. That's not theft. That's how every artist in history has developed their craft.

Looking back, I can see that this period, the Costco camera, the free wedding, the $300 trailer park job, the mentor who opened doors and the husband who tried to slam them shut, was never about becoming a photographer. It was about becoming someone who creates herself.

I didn't find myself during those years. I wasn't wandering around waiting to discover some hidden truth about who I was supposed to be. I was building. Choice by choice, job by job, technique by technique, I was constructing the person I wanted to become.

You don't find yourself. You create yourself.

The girl who walked into that photography class junior year was not the same person who walked out of that street fair after being screamed at. She had been forged by the work. Changed by the choices. Strengthened by the setbacks.

And she was just getting started.

* * *

[THE LESSON]: Create Yourself, Don't Find Yourself

Stop searching for yourself as if you are lost. You are not here to find yourself; you are here to create yourself.

Life is not about discovering some hidden version of who you're supposed to be. It's about consciously building the person you want to become through daily choices, actions, and intentions.

When I made those $25 payments on my camera, I was creating myself as someone who earns what she wants. When I shot that first wedding for free, I was creating myself as someone willing to start ugly. When I didn't quit after the street fair, I was creating myself as someone who keeps going.

Every choice is an act of creation. Every action shapes who you're becoming.

The deeper truth: People just treat you like you treat you. Everything around you that you allow for yourself speaks loud and clear, the boundaries you set, the space you've created for yourself, the work you do, the people you spend time with. When I walked into that photographer's studio and offered to work for free, I was treating myself like someone worth investing in. When I didn't quit after being screamed at, I was treating myself like someone who doesn't give up. And the world responded accordingly.

Don't wait to find yourself. Create yourself. Start today.

[YOUR TURN]

Describe the person you want to create yourself into. Not who you think you should be. Not who other people expect you to be. Who do you want to become? What values does she hold? How does she carry herself? What work does she do? How does she handle setbacks? Be specific. Be bold.

What is your "first click" moment? When did something feel different for you, even if you dismissed it at the time? When did you try something new and think: This. This feels like me.

What would you do today if you were willing to start ugly? What dream have you been putting off because you don't feel ready? What first step have you been avoiding because it's not glamorous enough, not perfect enough, not impressive enough?

Finally: What have you declared that The Voice told you was impossible? What did you say out loud that The Voice immediately tried to crush? Write it down. That declaration isn't crazy. It's the first draft of your future.

34

3

Hungry to Learn

Before I tell you about college, let me tell you about the magazines.

When I was eleven or twelve years old, my best friend, Lizzie and I would scrape together whatever change we could find and walk to the market to buy fashion magazines. Vogue. Elle. Glamour. Whatever we could afford. Top Model if we really saved. We'd go to Payless Market with a couple of dollars and pick out whatever fashion magazine we could afford, then head back home and digest that thing cover to cover.

Her and I were a couple of poor kids from a small town who had no business caring about haute couture or runway lighting or editorial spreads. But we didn't know that. We just knew those magazines were magic.

We'd sit together for hours, turning pages, tearing out the photos we loved. We'd talk about the fashion, the models, the posing, the lighting, the backdrops. We studied those images like scholars studying scripture. We lived inside those pages. We would create our own art books with the photos, basically creating our own magazines. We tore out our favorite photos, the photos of our favorite models, and we studied everything about them.

For two girls from Lockeford with holes in their clothes and dirt on our shoes, those magazines were a window into a world that seemed impossibly far away. A world of beauty and creativity and intention, where every image meant something, where every detail was chosen.

I didn't know yet that I wanted to create that world. I just knew I wanted to be inside it. That hunger never left me.

When it came time for college, my mom suggested I check out Delta College. But I told her, "Mom, I don't want to go where all the other kids are going. I don't want to go where all the kids I know from school are going, all the poor kids from my school. I don't want to feel poor and I don't want to feel lost. And I don't want to feel the same. I want to feel different."

So I went north until I hit Cosumnes River College. It wasn't Stanford. It wasn't some prestigious art school on the East Coast with ivy-covered buildings and a six-figure price tag. It was a community college in Sacramento with one of the best photography programs in the state of California. And it changed my life.

I dropped in and looked at everything they had to offer. They had state-of-the-art labs, state-of-the-art printing setups, color, black and white, everything I could ever possibly want to do. They had an extensive darkroom and color lab, printing area, everything for finishing prints, and a pretty extensive list of classes.

I met Jim West, who ran that program, and I just knew that's where I was going to go. I came home excited and told my mom about all the photography classes they had, showed her the catalog, told her this is where I'm going. And the day I left to go to my first day at school, I turned back to her and said, "Someday I'm going to own my own magazine, Mom."

Power of intention. Power of thought. Power of your words. Watch what you say. It shapes your reality.

I was eighteen years old when I started in 2000, fresh out of high school, finally finding my place. I remember the first day I walked into the photography lab. The smell hit me first, the chemicals, the developers, that sharp, specific scent that meant work is happening here. Then I saw the printing machines, the enlargers, the photos hanging everywhere. Student work. Teacher work. History.

Something in my chest unlocked. This was it. This was the place I'd been looking for without knowing I was looking. For the first time in my academic life, I wasn't bored. I wasn't struggling. I wasn't watching the clock and counting the minutes until I could leave. I was leaning in, hungry, wanting more. I couldn't get enough of it.

We studied the history of photography, the masters, the

movements, the evolution from daguerreotype to digital. We learned technique: composition, lighting, exposure, the alchemy of the darkroom. We critiqued each other's work, learned to see with new eyes, learned to make images that meant something. And I was good at it. For the first time, everything I did, I excelled at. The girl who failed English, who was average at everything, who never quite fit, she was an A-plus student here. She belonged.

So I became a straight-A student, and I wanted to be at school every single day. And I was. I never missed class, never, because I loved it so much. With the photography program, you also had media. So there were writing classes, journalism classes, film classes, all these things I was exposed to and had to learn. But I absolutely loved all of it.

My teachers saw something in me. Jim West. Patty Felkner. Dean Takuno. These weren't just instructors collecting a paycheck; they were working photographers who believed in craft, who invested in their students, who treated us like future colleagues rather than kids filling seats. They started teaching me commercial photography, portrait photography, fine art photography, and fashion photography.

Dean Takuno would talk about his fashion studio, sleek and sexy, booked solid all year. He'd describe the work, the clients, the lifestyle, and I'd sit there thinking: I could do that. That could actually be me. He was talking about his studio in the big city and how he was getting day rates of $10,000 a day. That just opened so many doors in my mind. The mind that was told that I couldn't do it, right? That little Voice that said

I'd never make money taking photos. Well, I was learning from people that not only said that was wrong, but they were doing the things that proved that theory wrong.

He made it real. Not a fantasy, not a pipe dream, but an actual career path that actual people walked. People who started somewhere, just like I was starting. The hunger grew.

I started taking fashion classes. And suddenly, all those magazines my best friend and I had torn apart as kids made sense in a new way. I wasn't just looking at pretty pictures anymore; I was understanding how they were made. The lighting setups. The composition choices. The relationship between photographer and subject. Those pages I'd lived inside as a poor kid from Lockeford? I was learning to create them.

As I was photographing some of my free sessions, I was taking them to my lab in college and I was developing the film and the prints. I was learning how to print on that fine art paper. Then I would take them back to my house, to my little room in Lockeford. I had an art desk set up. It was tiny, a tiny, tiny room with an art desk and a bed and all my oil paints. I would stay up late at night hand tinting these photos.

It was magnificent. It was artistic. It was beautiful. It was creative. It was fun. It ignited the correct side of my brain. And I fell deeply in love with photography. Deeply. I would take my film to school and my teachers would help me and critique me. We had live subjects and we learned posing and artistic form and composition. And I couldn't get enough.

Here's what nobody told me about education: it doesn't have to look the way they say it should. I was still struggling with English. Still fighting for C+ and B- while I sailed through photography with straight A's. And for a while, that felt like proof that I was broken, good at one thing, bad at the thing that "mattered."

But then I had a teacher named Kris. She was my English teacher, and unlike the others who'd marked up my papers with red ink and sighs of disappointment, Kris actually took time with me. She sat with me. She taught me about structure, not as a prison, but as a tool. And somewhere in those conversations, I started to understand something about myself.

The problem wasn't that I couldn't write. The problem was that traditional English classes didn't let me color outside the lines. Everything had to fit a formula. Five paragraphs. Thesis statement here. Supporting evidence there. Conclusion that restates what you already said. I've never been good with that kind of structure. I've never been good at following recipes someone else wrote.

I'm a cook, not a baker. When you bake, you have to follow the rules exactly. Too much flour, the cake falls. Wrong temperature, the bread doesn't rise. Baking is chemistry, and chemistry demands precision. But cooking? Cooking is jazz. You taste as you go. You adjust. You throw in a little of this, a little of that. You make it up as you move, and somehow it works. You create something that never existed before, and it's yours. (Just like this book).

I'm a cook. I always have been. I make my own rules. I create as I go. And when someone tells me I have to do it their way, something in me rebels. That's not a flaw. That's who I am.

Kris helped me see that. She didn't try to turn me into a baker. She just helped me find enough structure to get through the class while leaving room for me to be myself. It was the first time an English teacher met me where I was instead of demanding I become someone else. She would listen when I said I don't like your rules. And she'd say, "Okay, let's explore this." I got through it mostly because I was excited to be in school every day for the photography classes.

Years later, this experience would inform how I chose to educate my own son, understanding that traditional classroom structure isn't the only path to mastery, that some people need room to create their own way forward.

While I was in school in 2001, I got a job at a senior portrait studio. Not the hand-tinting photographer from before, this was something different. A commercial operation. A machine. They were shooting fifty to a hundred seniors per day. Not per week. Per day. And they were making anywhere from $500 to $2,000 per session.

I watched that operation like a hawk. This wasn't art photography; this was business photography. Systems. Efficiency. Volume. They had it dialed in: the poses, the lighting setups, the sales process, the turnaround time. Everything was designed to move.

The Voice had always told me: You'll never make money taking pictures. Photography is a hobby, not a career. Get a real job.

But here I was, watching people make serious money taking pictures. Not theoretical money. Real money, every single day, fifty to a hundred times a day. The bullshit I'd been fed my whole life, that I couldn't do this, that I needed to work for someone else, that I needed a "real" job with health insurance and a 401k, it crumbled right there in that senior portrait studio.

These people had debunked The Voice. They were living proof that everything I'd been told was wrong. I was so in love with what I was doing that I wasn't going to stop. Not for The Voice. Not for anyone's expectations. Not for the safe path that everyone said I should take. I was going to figure out how to make money doing what I loved.

I worked there for about a year, absorbing their systems, understanding how high-volume photography businesses actually worked. And the whole time, I was building my own client base on the side, shooting weddings and portraits for myself, learning to run my own sessions, my own way. I was taking senior portraits, taking small weddings that I could handle. And by year two, I was definitely starting to take sessions, and my photography was getting better and better.

My entire education, photography classes, English classes, all of it, cost me less than $5,000. Let me say that again: under five thousand dollars. I didn't go into debt. I didn't spend four years at an expensive university collecting credentials. I went to a community college, learned from masters, worked alongside professionals, and built the foundation of everything I would become, for less than the cost of a used car. I took a very cheap education and I wrung the shit out of it and got every drop and every ounce of information I could ever get out of it and every ounce of enjoyment I could ever get out of that education.

Understand that education, it can come from anywhere. It doesn't have to look the way they tell you it should look. It doesn't have to cost what they tell you it should cost. It doesn't have to follow the path they prescribe. You can write your own damn story.

You can pick it how you want, paint it as you want. It might be messy. It might not make sense at first. But you'll figure it out. The key is hunger. Not credentials. Not money. Not the "right" school or the "right" connections. Hunger.

I walked into Cosumnes River College with hunger, and I walked out with mastery. Not because the school gave it to me, but because I took everything they offered and demanded more. I learned in class and after class. I worked at the senior portrait studio and watched how business actually worked. I studied the magazines I'd loved as a kid and figured out how those images were made. Nobody handed me anything. I was hungry, and I chased it.

There's one more thing I learned during this time, something that would guide me for the rest of my career: Always align yourself with the very best. From the very beginning, I knew that was the way. When I wanted to learn hand-tinting, I found the best photographer in town and knocked on her door. When I wanted to learn photography formally, I found the best program I could access. When I wanted to understand the business side, I got a job at a studio that was actually making money.

I didn't try to figure it out alone. I didn't assume I already knew what I needed to know. I found people who were where I wanted to be, and I got as close as possible. It's about learning from excellence. It's about understanding that the fastest way to grow is to surround yourself with people who are already doing what you dream of doing.

You can read all the books you want. But nothing replaces proximity to mastery. Find the best. Get close. Watch everything. Ask questions. Work for free if you have to. That's how you learn. That's how you grow. That's how you build something from nothing.

* * *

[THE LESSON]: Mastery Gives Value Education Cannot

Credentials are junk paper. Mastery is power.

No one can take your mastery away from you. Not The Voice. Not the people who doubt you. Not the circumstances you were born into. Once you've put in the work, once you've built the skill, it's yours forever.

They say it takes 10,000 hours of quality time to master something. That's not a weekend seminar or a six-week online course. That's years of showing up, doing the work, failing, adjusting, and doing it again.

You can't fake mastery. You can fake credentials, buy a degree, pad a resume, talk a good game. But you can't fake the ability to actually do the work.

Education opens doors. Mastery walks through them.

Here's something else I learned: Practice until it's easy. I feel the same energy in my body today as I did the first time I walked on stage. But now I've practiced so much that my content is in my frontal lobe, it flows out of me because I've been writing and practicing. Beta testing is practice. Workshops are practice. Practice until it's easy.

[YOUR TURN]

Where have you put in your 10,000 hours? What have you mastered through dedication and practice? It doesn't have to be a career skill, it could be parenting, cooking, gardening, problem-solving, surviving. Where have you done the work?

What shame have you been carrying that could become your greatest strength? I carried the shame of failing English for years. It felt like proof that I was broken. But that "weakness" pushed me toward photography, toward visual storytelling, toward a career I never would have found if I'd been good at essays. What shame are you carrying? What if it's not a flaw, what if it's a signpost pointing you toward your actual path?

Are you a cook or a baker? Do you thrive within structure, or do you need room to create? Are you following someone else's recipe, or are you making it up as you go? There's no wrong answer. But knowing which one you are changes everything about how you should approach your goals.

4

Stockton

My father had concerns about photography as my only income source. He'd grown up poor, had watched his own family struggle, and he wanted me to have security. Multiple streams of income. A backup plan.

"Get your real estate license," he told me. "You can still do photography, but you need something that guarantees a paycheck." He'd told me photographers will starve to death. That I won't make ten cents as an artist. That I needed to do something productive.

He was teaching me to be practical, to protect myself. And looking back now, I can see he was right.

So I did. While I was finishing up at Cosumnes River College in 2002, I added real estate classes in the evenings, same campus, different building. I got my license. And in 2003, fresh out of school, I dove into real estate. I never stopped shooting photos; I was always taking sessions when I could get them. But real estate became my day job, my "responsible" choice, my answer to everyone who said photography wasn't practical.

The Voice loved this decision. See? This is smart. This is safe. This is what grown-ups do. You can always do photography on the side, but you need something real to pay the bills.

But there was another voice too, quieter, deeper, harder to ignore. My heart hungered for more. And somewhere beneath all the practical choices and responsible decisions, I had an intuitive knowing: I would be successful at whatever I did. It might take a while. I might have to work really hard and get beat up along the way. But I knew I would eventually make it. I just didn't know yet what "it" would be.

I hated real estate. Back-biting, ass-beating, dog-eat-dog. But I found one of my greatest mentors through it.

I ended up in Stockton, California. Not the nice parts of Stockton, if there were nice parts, I never saw them. I was working in the shittiest part of Stockton, taking the listings nobody else wanted, cold calling the neighborhoods everyone else avoided. It was just a newspaper ad I saw where a broker was taking new agents and doing some training. Nobody guided me on it. I had to figure out how to maneuver that myself.

The surface streets were okay. You could drive through, do your business, get out. But once you dug deeper into Stockton, you found yourself in a different world.

I remember door knocking in neighborhoods where literal gun fights were happening on the streets. Not on the news. Right there, while I was walking up to someone's porch with my clipboard and my smile and my pitch about listing their property.

These were the people saying yes to us off cold calls. The ones who picked up the phone when we dialed. The ones who wanted to sell. And someone had to go meet them, and that someone was usually me, because I was new and hungry and didn't know enough to say no.

I was young. I was beautiful, which sounds like a blessing until you're walking through a rough neighborhood and every man on the block is whistling at you, hollering at you. I called my dad one night and told him: "I don't feel safe."

And I didn't. I was in situations I had no business being in, with no real guidance about what I should or shouldn't be doing. I was just thrown into it, sink or swim, figure it out, close the deal or don't get paid.

Looking back, I'm lucky nothing ever happened. But something did happen, even if it wasn't the kind of thing that makes the news. My eyes opened.

I thought I grew up poor. I thought Lockeford, with our clothes with holes and vegetables from the garden, was what poverty looked like. Then I saw parts of Stockton. And I realized that compared to some of these neighborhoods, I had lived like a king. The contrast was staggering. It taught me something about perspective, about how much I actually had, even when I thought I had nothing.

It also taught me to be brave. When you've knocked on doors in neighborhoods where gun fights break out, when you've walked into situations that should have scared you away but didn't, when you've learned to hold your ground even when everything in you wants to run, you come out different on the other side. Stockton didn't make me a great real estate agent. But it made me tougher than I'd ever been.

And then there was John.

I ended up going to my first day in the middle of Stockton for my introduction meeting. I met an old gray-haired man with a big nose and his partner, who was a large man with this fun voice and this amazing spirit. We were connected right away.

John was my broker, and he was unlike anyone I'd ever met. Big guy. Chain smoker. Grew up in the worst part of Stockton himself, street smart in ways that couldn't be taught in any classroom. He drove a Cadillac Escalade, wore three-piece suits, and knew how to sell like it was a language he'd been born speaking.

He'd become a top producer in the shittiest part of Stockton. Think about that. He'd taken the worst territory, the hardest clients, the deals nobody else wanted, and he'd built an empire from it.

The whole agency was like that. We were an office of misfits. Nobody there fit the mold of what a "successful" real estate agent was supposed to look like. But we were high-producing misfits, beating everyone else by sheer numbers, by a system of sales that was relentless and effective.

We actually had a call center and we had to be there from 9 to noon. We had call lists and we were expected to call over 200 people every morning and read scripts. Cold calling by the masses. Practicing in sales groups. Learning to read people and situations. There was a whole program for it, and John taught me all of it.

I learned scripts. I learned how to write them. I learned how to project them. I learned tonality in the scripts. I learned how to sell.

But here's what made John different from every other mentor I'd ever have: sales was just the surface. Everything John taught was really about the mind.

He was a graduate of neurolinguistic programming, and not just a graduate, but a decorated instructor. What they teach you in neurolinguistic programming is to find common ground with your subject immediately and develop rapport through certain techniques in your language and in your body.

He taught me about positive thinking, not the fluffy, wishful kind, but the disciplined practice of directing your thoughts toward what you want instead of what you fear. He taught me about reading people. Body language. Tonality. The things people say without saying. The things they want without knowing they want them.

He put me through courses that helped me develop as a student. He put me through sales courses. I learned how to understand contracts. I learned how to get beat up. I learned how to negotiate. I learned how to be a businesswoman. And let me tell you, these son of a bitches that beat me up and took deals from me while I was a youngster, taught me how to throw elbows, and I thank them for it now.

John was also a certified hypnotherapist. He ended up doing some hypnotherapy sessions with me, some timeline work, and helped me break through some old trauma stuff that I had. I got a lot out of that dumpy-ass office in Stockton.

And he taught me about emotional mastery.

That phrase would follow me for the rest of my life. Emotional mastery. The ability to feel what you feel without being controlled by it. The ability to stay steady when everything around you is chaos. The ability to respond instead of react.

One afternoon, he pulled me aside after a training session. "Dee, most people think sales is about convincing someone to buy. It's not. It's about managing your own mind so you can read theirs."

He tapped his temple. "When you're desperate, people smell it. When you're afraid, they feel it. When you master your emotions, when you can stay steady no matter what they say, you become powerful."

That lesson served me in every negotiation, every business deal, every moment someone tried to make me feel small for the next twenty years.

John didn't just teach me how to close a deal. He taught me how to manage myself. And that skill, that deep, psychological understanding of my own mind, that followed into every relationship and every business I ever built. He brought all of our office to retreats, motivational conventions. Those things changed my life. I didn't even know they existed. I learned the power of setting goals and intentions and pushing. It was life-changing.

I think of him often. I've never had another mentor like him.

I was in his office one afternoon and I was telling him how discouraged I was with a customer. He let me go on and on, as immature minds usually do and when I finally took a pause, he just looked at me and knocked over his glass of water all over his desk. It was obviously intentional so I didn't react too much, but it made uncomfortable. My instict was to help him clean it up and the mess itself made me antsy. He never broke eye contact, and he said, "How does that make you feel?" I said "Well shit, I don't know… I guess a little anxious." He let it sit there a little longer before grabbing the paper towels behind him. Then he said "You are choosing the emotion you are attaching to that action. It is your choice. You could have laughed and felt it was funny or cried and felt it was sad, but bottom line, its your choice." I sat there quietly. Self mastery. He was showing me that what I was experiencing in the business deal that I complaining to him about was fully in my control.

He went on and said, "Have you ever been in a diner and the waitress came around during breakfast and ofered you coffee?" "Well, yes of course." I replied. "have you ever turned her down and said 'no'?"

"Yes, of course"

"Do you think she went in the back room and statred crying about you turning her down?"

"That's silly, of course not." I said.

"Do you think she went to her boss and complained about the customer saying 'no'?"
I sat there quietly. "Received." I said. "Thank you for that."

Then he just sat back in his chair and said "Anytime."
And he meant it. He was always there to guide me in business and I'll never forget that lesson.

Time went on and I was about twenty-one, twenty-two years old, this was 2003, 2004, somewhere in there. Single. In good shape. No bills to speak of, no one to hold me accountable. I came and went as I pleased.

John wanted every agent in the office full-time. That was the expectation. You showed up, you worked the phones, you went on appointments, you closed deals. All day, every day. But I was young, and I didn't always follow the rules. (I STILL DONT!)

One afternoon, I walked into the office after being gone for two hours. I'd been at a spin class. I was freshly showered, feeling good, ready to put in an afternoon session. John was out front, smoking a cigarette. He looked at me.

"Where were you?"

"I was at the gym," I said. "For like two hours."

He took a drag, nodded slowly. "I bet you're feeling great."

"I am."

He was quiet for a moment. Then he said something I didn't expect. "You know, something inside me tells me this doesn't make you happy every day."

I stopped. He was right. I was making good money. I was learning incredible skills. But real estate wasn't my calling. It wasn't what made me come alive. The problem I had with real estate, as far as the resale market went, is it wasn't creative.

"What are you going to do instead?" he asked.

"Photography," I said. "I want to build a photography business."

He nodded. Took another drag. And then he said the words that changed everything: "Then you should go."

Not: "You're being irresponsible." Not: "You need to stick it out." Not: "Photography isn't practical."

Just: "Then you should go."

He wasn't firing me, but he was definitely letting me go. He gave me permission to leave. Permission I didn't know I needed but had been waiting for anyway. He knew I felt obligated to show up there every day. But I couldn't do it. I didn't want to do it. And I wasn't happy. And he knew.

I stayed a little longer, long enough to finish out my commitments, to close my deals, to do it right. I stayed through the end of 2004, then transitioned out. By 2005, I was focusing on photography full-time.

In May 2005, I met Ronnie. He wasn't in real estate or photography. He was solid, steady, the kind of man who saw me for who I was and loved all of me. He didn't try to talk me out of my dreams or convince me to play it safe. He just showed up, day after day, believing in me even when I wasn't sure I believed in myself.

We got married two years later, in 2007, right before everything would change.

Here's what I learned in Stockton that I didn't expect to learn: Sometimes the "practical" choice is training for the dream.

My father wanted me to have something to fall back on. He was trying to protect me. And in a way, he was right; I did need skills beyond photography to build what I wanted to build. But not for the reasons he thought.

Real estate didn't become my fallback. It became my foundation. The skills John taught me, reading people, emotional mastery, understanding contracts, managing my mind under pressure, those skills didn't just help me sell houses. They helped me negotiate with clients, manage difficult personalities, close business deals, protect myself legally, and build multiple businesses from the ground up. In the span of years working for him, I learned a tremendous amount of business. And meanwhile, I was building my photography business and implementing a lot of the things I was learning.

Years later, after I'd built my photography business and bought my first magazine business and was standing in rooms with people who thought I didn't belong, I'd think about John. About Stockton. About the neighborhoods where I learned to be brave and the office where I learned to be strategic.

My father's guidance to get that real estate license wasn't about giving up on photography; it was about becoming someone capable of building an empire. And John, John saw it before any of us did.

Looking back, I can see that Stockton was never about real estate. It was about becoming someone who could do hard things. Someone who could walk into dangerous neighborhoods and not flinch. Someone who could cold call strangers and handle rejection. Someone who could read a room and understand what people needed before they said it. Someone who could master her own emotions even when everything around her was chaos. And someone who got roughed up by the seasoned agents daily and still got up off the mat to fight another day.

That's who I needed to be to build what was coming next. Photography was the dream. But I couldn't have built the business I wanted to build without the foundation John gave me in Stockton.

I was always shooting photos on the side, always taking sessions when I could get them. But building a photography business from scratch, with no marketing tools except referrals and reputation, that was a slow climb. Real estate bridged the gap. It paid the bills while I built the dream.

And John, John gave me the skills to succeed at both.

* * *

[THE LESSON]: Master the Paperwork and Study the Room

The world runs on contracts and documents. Learn the paper. It will save you.

This sounds boring. It's not glamorous. But I cannot tell you how many times understanding paperwork has protected me. How many deals I've caught before they went sideways. How many negotiations I've won because I knew exactly what I was signing.

Contracts are not optional. Signatures are not formalities. Every document you sign is a promise, and every promise has consequences. Learn the paper. Understand what you're agreeing to. It's not paranoia; it's protection.

I worked with another agent who was cutthroat. I can't tell you how many times she reminded me, as she was taking deals off my desk, that I didn't have the contract signed. I got really good at contracts and getting the signatures on things and dotting the i's and crossing the t's. You better have the ink on the paper, because some people will cut your throat at any cost.

Photography taught me to see people. Real estate taught me to read them.

When you can read people, really read them, you negotiate better. You protect your interests faster. You know when to push and when to walk away. You catch the liars before they burn you.

This isn't manipulation. It's awareness. It's paying attention. Stay sharp. Study the room. Trust your gut when something feels off.

[YOUR TURN]

What unexpected education have you received? Maybe it was a job you didn't love. Maybe it was a relationship that taught you hard lessons. Maybe it was a season of your life that felt like a detour but turned out to be training. What did you learn in the places you didn't expect to learn?

____

____

____

____

____

Who has been your John? Who saw you, really saw you, and gave you permission to follow your path? Who invested in you as a person, not just as a means to their end? If you haven't had a John yet, what would you want that mentor to teach you?

____

____

____

____

____

What paperwork do you need to master? Is there an area of your life or business where you've been avoiding the details? Contracts you sign without reading? Financial documents you don't understand? Legal agreements you hope will just work out?

____

____

____

____

____

____

5

Before the Fall

I learned early that if you want something, you have to ask for it. Not hope for it. Not wait for it. Not drop hints and pray someone notices. You have to open your mouth, say what you want, and see what happens.

This has become a pattern in my life. I don't skip a beat. When I see an opportunity, I ask.

It was 2007. I'd married Ronnie that year, this solid, steady man who saw me for who I was and loved me anyway. He'd been in construction since the early 90s, building custom homes for NFL players in the Bay Area. He'd been at it for twenty years. He came from that area, he was well-networked. By the time we met in 2005, he owned a beautiful ranch and his business was booked solid, two and a half years ahead. The kind of backlog that meant security, stability, success. When I moved into his ranch, our ranch then, with the animals and the space and the life he'd worked so hard to build, we were just a couple of poor kids from the Central Valley who thought we'd finally made it.

There was a designer friend I had known most of my life. She was talented, successful, running high-end projects for hotels and commercial spaces. And she needed engagement photos. So she hired me. We did the shoot. It went beautifully. The images captured exactly what she wanted, intimate, romantic, polished. And then, almost as an afterthought, she mentioned something.

"I'm working on these hotel projects. Big spaces. They need artwork for the walls, large-scale photography, original pieces. It's hard to find what we're looking for."

My brain clicked into gear immediately. This is an opportunity. I didn't skip a beat. I took one split second to say, "Who's doing the artwork, the creative artwork, to go into these hotels?"

And that is the very split second that you have to say what you want.

"Use me," I said. "I want to be your artist. You tell me what you need, I will provide it. I've got photos. Fine art portfolios. Let's meet. Look at your designs, and I'll show you what I have. If it fits, great. If not, I can shoot something custom for you."

She paused. Looked at me. "Really?"

"Absolutely. When can we meet?"

If I didn't speak up, if I let fear grab my tongue, I would have never got that opportunity.

Three days later, I was sitting in her office with my portfolio spread across the table. She went through image after image, landscapes, abstracts, moody black-and-whites, vibrant color studies. Work I'd shot over years, not knowing what I'd do with it, just creating because I loved it.

And she said yes. Not to one piece, but to thousands of pieces. To multiple projects. Hotels across California that needed original artwork.

The first project was a boutique hotel in Sacramento, 1,800 pieces total. I had a huge learning curve. I had to learn all kinds of things about construction and design and large batch ordering of prints, matting and framing of large batch orders. Each piece was a minimum of $1,000 each, and more in the range of $1,500 each. I shot custom California landscapes: vineyards at sunset, coastal rock formations, Sierra meadows. Each image was printed, professionally framed, and installed. The project paid upwards of $150,000. For photography. For work I loved doing.

Within six months, I had three more hotels. Then a restaurant. Then a medical office building. The commercial work was steady, repeatable, and lucrative. And it taught me something crucial: The bigger the client, the bigger the budget. The bigger the problem you solve, the more you get paid.

I asked for what I wanted, sitting in a wedding meeting. I started the projects at 25 years old, finished them at 26, and made over half a million dollars in my studio from that opportunity alone. And I just had a newborn baby.

That designer connection opened a door I didn't even know existed. Suddenly I was shooting for hotels. For commercial spaces. For clients who had budgets that made everything else look small. Large-scale prints. Custom framing. Installations that would be seen by thousands of people. This wasn't wedding photography. This wasn't portraits. This was commercial work at scale.

My photography business was growing. Commercial hotel projects bringing in significant income. Weddings and portraits filling in the gaps. My calendar was booking months in advance. I had confidence. I had a reputation. Clients referred other clients. Hotels hired me for multiple projects.

Ronnie's construction business was equally strong. Booked years ahead. Bringing in consistent, reliable income. We had the ranch. The animals. The space. The life.

And then in July 2008, after seventy-six hours of labor, Rowdy was born.

Seventy-six hours. Three full days of my body trying to bring this baby into the world, fighting through exhaustion and pain and fear. When he finally arrived, when they put him on my chest and I looked into his face for the first time, I felt something I'd never felt before. Purpose. Not the kind of purpose you find in work or achievement. The kind that rewrites everything you thought you knew about who you are and what matters.

I was a mother now.   Ronnie and I were new parents, navigating this together. And everything, every decision, every risk, every move forward, would be filtered through that new reality.

I was in deep motherhood fog those first months. Breastfeeding around the clock. Learning how to keep a tiny human alive. Figuring out sleep schedules and diaper changes and all the things nobody actually prepares you for. My photography business was still running. I was shooting weddings and portraits out of our home, managing clients between feedings, editing photos during Rowdy's naps. I was in some mom groups and I was photographing moms' babies and family sessions. It wasn't the workload I was doing before, but I had some business going on.

We thought we were untouchable. We thought we'd finally made it.

But there were warnings. Small signs that something was shifting beneath the surface.

I remember one particular conversation with a real estate agent, a seasoned woman who'd been in the business for decades. We were at an open house. I still had my license then, even though photography was my main focus. She pulled me aside.

"You see all this?" she said, gesturing to the crowd of people touring the expensive home. "The bidding wars? The prices going up and up?"

I nodded.

"This is a bubble," she said quietly. "And it's going to pop. I've seen it before. I'll see it again. Be smart. Don't overextend. Save everything you can. Because when it crashes, and it will crash, you want to be ready."

I heard her. But I didn't really listen. Because everything around me said the opposite. The market was hot. Work was plentiful. Money was flowing. Why would I prepare for a crash that might never come?

Ronnie's ranch had an adjustable rate mortgage, an ARM. One of those mortgages where the interest rate adjusts after a set period. He'd bought it years before we met. It seemed fine at the time. Everyone was doing it. The payments were manageable. Nobody explained what would happen when the rate adjusted. Or maybe they did, and we didn't understand. We were young. We trusted the system.

And then, in 2008, the rate adjusted.

Our mortgage payment doubled. Not gradually. Not over time. Just boom. Double.

Adjustable rate mortgages. A scam for pirates to take your shit. That's what that means.

Suddenly the ranch that had felt affordable, the dream we'd worked so hard for, became a financial noose tightening around our necks.

But we still had income. Ronnie was still booked. I was still shooting. We thought we could handle it. We thought if we just worked harder, saved more, tightened the budget, we could make it work. We had no idea what was coming.

The housing market crashed in late 2008. And when it crashed, it took everything with it.

Ronnie's construction business, went to zero. Not slow. Not gradual. Zero. Every contract fell through. Every project got canceled. Every client who'd been ready to build suddenly wasn't. The phone stopped ringing. The work dried up. And we were left standing there with a doubled mortgage payment and no income.

My photography business held on a little longer. But the hotel projects stopped. Budgets froze. New construction halted. The commercial work that had been bringing in significant income dried up almost overnight.

Weddings started canceling too. People who'd been planning celebrations suddenly couldn't afford them. Portraits got postponed. Nobody was spending money on anything that wasn't absolutely essential. And photography, no matter how good, no matter how meaningful, wasn't essential. Not when people were losing their homes.

We spent the next two years burning through every dollar we'd saved, trying to keep the ranch. We fought through 2009, into 2010, and nearly to 2011. Our retirement accounts. Our savings. Everything. We invested all of our money, everything we had into saving that house for another two years. We didn't know it was unsavable. We didn't know that no amount of fighting would be enough. We just kept throwing money at it, hoping we could bail fast enough to keep it afloat. We couldn't.

It was grim. We were picking up small jobs here and there, both of us. Small, portrait jobs for me. Ronnie was picking up things like building someone's deck in Monterey, traveling three hours to pick up a small job to survive.

The notices started coming. We read them, knowing we couldn't pay. We watched it building like a tsunami on the horizon, this massive wave coming for us, and there was nothing we could do to stop it. So we held hands. We held our breath. And we went under when it crashed over us.

By early 2011, we lost the ranch. Foreclosure. The words that had seemed impossible just a few years earlier when everything was booming.

Shame, shame, shame.

There's a moment, right before you lose everything, when you can see it coming but you can't stop it. You're standing on the beach, watching the water pull back, back, back. And you know what that means. You know what's coming. But you can't run. You can't move. You can only stand there and wait for it to hit.

That's what 2008-2011 felt like. Watching everything we'd built get pulled away. Knowing we were about to lose it all. And being completely powerless to stop it.

Rowdy was not quite three years old when we had to leave the ranch. Just a baby, really. Too young to understand what was happening, but old enough to feel the tension. The stress. The fear that lived in our house during those final months. What we'd built? It was falling. And there was nothing we could do but survive the crash.

* * *

[THE LESSON]: Catch the Wave, But Know When to Get Off

Opportunity shows up when you ask for it. That designer didn't offer me the hotel work. I asked for it. I didn't wait to be invited. I didn't hope she'd think of me. I saw an opening, and I asked: "How can I help you? How can I bring value to this project?" And she said yes.

Ask for what you want. There's no other way to put it. If you have goals and you have opportunity, you cannot be afraid to ask for it. That is literally what has propelled me into success, learning to ask for what I want. And when the opportunity arises, you cannot question it and you cannot say no because you asked for it. You have to say yes and you have to lean into it.

This is about networking deep, building real relationships with people who are doing things you want to do. It's about showing up with value, not need. It's about asking: "How can I solve your problem?" instead of "Will you help me?"

The bigger the problem you solve, the more you get paid. Wedding photography paid well because I was solving an important problem: capturing one of the most significant days of people's lives. But commercial photography paid even better because I was solving a business problem: helping hotels create experiences for thousands of guests. Scale matters. Impact matters.

But here's what I know now that I didn't know then: When things are going well, that's when you prepare for things to go badly.

Booms don't last forever. Waves crash. Empires fall. Not because you did something wrong. Not because you failed. But because that's how markets work. That's how economies work. Nothing stays up forever.

The seasoned real estate agent tried to warn me. She saw the bubble forming. She knew it would pop. But I was young. I was confident. I was riding the wave. And I didn't prepare for the crash.

When you're making good money, save aggressively. When business is booming, build reserves. When the wave is carrying you up, start looking for the next wave, because this one will eventually crash.

Don't get comfortable. Don't get complacent. Ride the wave. Enjoy it. Make the most of it. But know when to get off.

[YOUR TURN]

What wave are you riding right now? What's going well in your business or life? Where is momentum carrying you forward? Write it down. Acknowledge it. Celebrate it.

____

____

____

____

____

____

Are you preparing for the crash? When things are going well, it's easy to assume they'll stay that way. But they won't.

Markets shift. Industries change. Circumstances evolve. What are you doing right now, while things are good, to prepare for when things get hard?

____

____

____

____

____

____

What opportunities are you not asking for? Who could you reach out to today and say: "How can I bring value to you? How can I solve your problem?" What doors could you open if you just asked?

____

____

____

____

6

Where We Went to Die

We lost our home in early 2011. It was absolutely devastating. Not just financially, though that was crushing enough. But emotionally. Spiritually. The weight of failure pressing down on us so hard I didn't know if we'd survive it.

Adjustable rate mortgages were designed to do exactly what they did, lure people in with low payments, then crush them when the rates adjusted. The housing market was built on speculation and greed and lies. And when it all came crashing down, the people who created the system walked away with golden parachutes. While families like mine lost everything.

I'm not looking for sympathy. I'm stating a fact. The game was rigged. And we played it because we didn't know any better.

After we lost the ranch, we had to find somewhere to go. Somewhere that would take us, a family with a foreclosure on record, and a collection of animals we refused to abandon.

We found a two-story rental house in the middle of nowhere. Calaveras County. Up in the foothills. Miles from anything that mattered. It was the only place that would have us.

The house was old. Worn. The kind of place nobody else wanted, which was exactly why we could afford it. But it had land. Space for the animals. Room to breathe. Ground to grow on. And it was ours, at least temporarily.

Later on I realized that it was the place where we went to die. The place where everything we knew, all of our old ways, and the false beliefs ended and our new way of living would be born. We made some big decisions about who we wanted to be spiritually in that period of time and after we were done there, everything changed.

Financial crisis, doesn't just threaten your bank account. It threatens everything. Your marriage. Your sanity. Your sense of self.

The number one driver of divorce in this country is financial stress. And in those years, Ronnie and I faced more tension, more pressure, more raw survival stress than most couples face in a lifetime.

We had a toddler. Rowdy was only about three when we lost the ranch. We were trying to keep a little boy's life stable while our entire world was collapsing around us.

We fought. God, we fought. Not about little things. About everything. About whose fault it was. About what we should have done differently. About whether we were going to make it. About whether we even wanted to make it.

It was so hard and I was so angry about losing everything. I was so depressed about the state of our business and everything that we had worked for being lost. A lot of shame around that.

The growth we had to go through just to stay together, just to keep fighting on the same team instead of against each other, that could be a whole book in itself. But we did it. We held on. Barely. But we did.

And I was fighting on another front too. One I didn't even recognize at the time.

Postpartum depression. It went on for years after Rowdy was born, and I didn't even know that's what it was. I just knew I was suffering. I knew something was wrong, but I couldn't name it. Couldn't ask for help. Couldn't admit that I was breaking.

Because I'd always been the strong one. The fighter. The one who got back up no matter what. But this time, I couldn't get up.

This was the lowest point of my life ever.

It was Christmas, Rowdy was four years old. Old enough to know what Christmas was supposed to be. Old enough to notice when it wasn't. We'd been in that rental house still scraping by. Still fighting. Still barely holding on.

And I was done.

I couldn't clean the house. Couldn't cook. Couldn't decorate. Couldn't even get off the couch. The house was a mess. No Christmas tree. No lights. No presents under a tree that didn't exist. I was lying on the couch, crying, unable to move. And I had nothing left to give.

I called my mom.

"I can't do it," I told her. "I can't get up. I can't go on. I don't know if I can make it another day. I don't think I have the strength."

She didn't ask questions. Didn't tell me to pull myself together. Didn't lecture me about being strong. She just said, "Okay, honey. I'll be right there."

My mother is an angel. She's always been an angel. Kind. Loving. The kind of woman who gives and gives and gives of herself, nurturing everyone around her without ever asking for anything in return.

She's the Christmas Queen. The holidays bring her pure joy, decorating, baking, wrapping presents, creating magic for the people she loves. And that day, she brought that magic to my broken life.

She drove up to our little rental house in the middle of nowhere. Walked in and saw the mess, dishes piled in the sink, laundry everywhere, me on the couch unable to move.

And she didn't say a word.

She just started working. She started my laundry. Washed the dishes. Cleaned the counters. Wiped down cabinets. Mopped the floors. Then she left. Drove to Home Depot. Came back with a Christmas tree, lights, ornaments. She went into my garage and found all my Christmas decorations, boxes I'd been too broken to open. She put up the tree. Strung the lights. Hung the ornaments. She had Christmas presents for Rowdy, wrapped them, put them under the tree. She laid out clean clothes for me. Drew me a bath. And she never said a word. Not one word of judgment. Not one question about why I couldn't do it myself. Not one comment about how I should be stronger or try harder or snap out of it. She just loved me. Through action. Through service. Through showing up when I couldn't show up for myself.

When everything was done, when the house was clean, the tree was up, the presents were wrapped, she came to the couch where I was still lying.

"Come on," she said gently. "I drew you a bath."

I let her lead me to the bathroom. Let her help me like I was a child again. When I came out, clean and dressed in the clothes she'd laid out, she had supper on the table. She fed me. She fed my family. She told me to rest. And then she left, not because she was done caring, but because she'd done what she came to do. She'd shown me I wasn't alone. She'd shown me I had foundation. Support. Someone who believed in me even when I didn't believe in myself.

Didn't say a word, didn't need words. That's the truest expression of love I've ever felt or saw from any human being ever.

That day taught me what unconditional love actually looks like. Not words. Not platitudes. Not "everything happens for a reason" or "just think positive." Action. Showing up. Doing what needs to be done without asking for credit or acknowledgment. Loving someone in their darkest moment without making them feel worse about being there.

My mother didn't fix my depression that day. She didn't solve my financial problems or save my marriage or make the shame go away. But she gave me something more important: She showed me I was worth fighting for. Even when I couldn't fight for myself.

I learned what love really is. I learned what pain really is. I learned what surviving really is. I learned how to get up off the mat that day. She believed in me. She had my back. She showed me I had foundation. She showed me I had support.

Now it was up to me to get up. Fight.

That Christmas was the turning point. Not immediately. Not dramatically. But slowly, over the weeks and months that followed, something shifted.

I started taking better care of myself. I started reaching out for help. I started teaching myself about natural health, about how what you put in your body affects everything about how you feel and function.

I dove deep into traditional healing methods. Practices I still use today. Growing food. Canning. Seed saving. Raising chickens and cattle. Building a life that could sustain itself.

I became obsessed with homesteading. With creating abundance from the land. With learning skills that our grandparents knew but our generation had forgotten. Giant gardens. An orchard. Preserving everything we grew.

It wasn't just about food. It was about control. About taking back some small piece of power in a life that felt completely out of control. If I couldn't control the economy or the housing market or whether we'd ever financially recover, I could control what we ate. How we lived. What we taught our son about self-sufficiency.

It saved me. Not all at once. But piece by piece, season by season, I came back to life.

Meanwhile, we were figuring out how to survive financially. We were on leased ground in Calaveras County. Land that didn't belong to us, but land we could use.

Ronnie had a friend who came over to see him and he said, "You know, you live in Calaveras County and you have the ability to farm very specific crops that are unregulated right now. If it were me, this is what I would do."

It was very gray. I still don't think it's a black and white situation, but it was a very gray situation. And I was shown opportunity to get up off the mat.

I'm very resourceful. My family is very resourceful. I'm very skilled. I can learn things very quickly. I learned how to diversify and survive. And that's what I did.

'I got up off the mat.' I learned a new trade. I learned a new skill. I learned how to implement a lot of my business sense in that trade. Including my elbow, throwing skills, I learned in Stockton. It gave me enough leverage to get to the next step and get to the next step and get to the next step and work again towards the goals I had set for myself.

I won't go into details. It's a story for another context. But what I will say is this: We learned to farm. We learned the business. And we used every dollar we made to rebuild.

The money wasn't huge at first. But it was steady. It taught me about diversification. About seeing opportunities others weren't seeing. About building something from absolutely nothing. We saved every penny. Lived lean. Reinvested smart. And in three years, exactly three years, we rebuilt our credit from destroyed to strong.

While all of this was unfolding, I was ready to make another move. I needed a photography studio. A real space. Not shooting out of my home anymore, I needed separation between work and life. I found a small house for rent on Pine Street in downtown Lodi. Beautiful area. Commercial district. The perfect location for a studio. But it was a wreck.

Carpet needed to be ripped up. Walls needed paint. The whole place needed a complete rehab to turn it into the vision I had in my head.

My father drove up to look at it. I was on my hands and knees, ripping up old carpet when he walked in. He stood there, looking around at the mess, at me covered in dust and sweat, at this broken-down space I was betting everything on.

And then he said, "You're out of your mind."
Turned around. And walked out.

The same pattern I'd seen before, the doubt, the silence, the tough-love. But I'd learned by then that I couldn't wait for his approval. Six months passed. Six months of me working on that studio anyway. Six months of me proving I could do this with or without his support.

And then he came back. Started showing up to help with the property whenever he could. The pattern repeated, doubt first, then action when he saw I was making it work. That studio became my sanctuary. The place where I could create again. Build again. Prove, to myself and everyone else, that I wasn't done.

I spent months rehabbing that building. Ripping up carpet, painting walls, building out my shooting space, my sales room, my systems. Making it beautiful. Making it mine. And then I had to build the business itself. New clients. New marketing. New everything. Starting from scratch, again. But this time, I did it differently. I wasn't just shooting sessions and handing over digital files anymore. I built a complete experience.

I'd learned from two very different photography studios years before, and I was about to combine everything they'd taught me. When I was eighteen, I'd worked for that boutique photographer, the one who did hand-tinted black and white portraits. She taught me about artistry, about creating heirloom pieces, about treating photography as fine art.

Then in my early twenties, I'd worked at that high-volume senior portrait studio. Fifty to a hundred sessions a day. Sales rooms running constantly. They taught me about systems, efficiency, and most importantly, how to sell.

I took the best of both worlds. The artistry and quality from the boutique studio. The sales systems and volume potential from the commercial studio. And I created something new.

Pre-consultation. The shoot. A sales meeting where I helped clients see the vision for their walls. I sold heirlooms. Art. Legacy pieces that would last generations. And I charged accordingly. But it didn't happen overnight. It took me a year, maybe a year and a half, to really dial in that system. To get the marketing right. To build the client base. To perfect the sales process. I had to learn through trial and error. Figure out what worked and what didn't. Refine everything until it was smooth.

By 2014, I had it dialed. $2,500 minimum. Most sessions $5,000 to $7,500. Some $10,000. Not because I was greedy. Because I'd learned my value. Because I'd survived losing everything and rebuilt from nothing. Because I refused to play small anymore. Word spread. My calendar filled up. The income returned. And slowly, so slowly, we climbed back up from the bottom.

The economy was beginning to turn around. I was picking up sessions again. Taking on weddings. Making five thousand, six thousand, seven thousand dollars a wedding. And that was growing. I was farming. I was making cash farming. I was making cash working as a photographer. I was saving. I was gaining ground.

And then, in 2015, something happened that changed every-thing.

We bought another ranch.

We did our time in 'purgatory' and we leaped. A bank-owned property that had been sitting abandoned for three years, just like us. Nobody wanted it. It was a disaster. A ranch that time had forgotten. But I saw potential. I could see what it could be and I could work towards it. That's one of my skillsets. I can see the vision. I can take things that look like nothing and make something great.

When I told my dad we were buying it, using money we'd saved and scraped together, he came to look at it. We drove in the driveway, and he took one look at it, and drove right back out and said "You're out of your mind!"

"You're going to what? Buy a ranch? An abandoned ranch?

Are you crazy?"

But we did it anyway. We bought that 1929 ranch. And we started rehabbing it. Slowly. One project at a time. Fixing what was broken. Building what was needed. Creating the life we wanted. It was a shithole. My dad drove in with me to see it. He drove right back out.

And at first, my dad stayed away. The familiar pattern playing out again. But then we started making progress. The house started looking better. The barn got repaired. The fences went up. The animals moved in. We were actually doing it. And that's when my dad showed up. Not with words. But with his tool belt and his truck and his hands ready to work.

He helped us. Taught Rowdy. Fixed things I didn't know how to fix. Spent weekends at the ranch working alongside us.

That ranch, the one he thought we were crazy to buy, became the place where he was most proud of me.

Years later, he'd sit on my back porch, watching the horses come in, the dogs running, the gardens growing. And he'd say: "Dee, buying this place was the best decision you ever made. That was the best buy you ever made. I'm so proud of you."

That's all I ever needed from him. To know he was proud of me.

Looking back now, I can see that those years in the rental house, "where we went to die," weren't the end. They were the transformation.

Everything we thought we were, all that vanity, the money, the status, the false beliefs about what mattered, it all had to die. So we could become who we actually needed to be. Stronger. Wiser. More resourceful. Less concerned with what other people thought. More focused on what we knew to be true, including God.

We didn't die there. We were reborn there.

And by 2015, we were ready to start building again. Not the same empire we'd lost. Something better. Something built on truth instead of illusion. On resilience instead of luck. On knowing we could survive anything, because we already had.

* * *

[THE LESSON]: Get Up Off the Mat

Nobody is coming to rescue you. When you're on the mat, bleeding, broken, wondering if you can survive, you have to rescue yourself.

My mother showed up with unconditional love through action, not words. She didn't fix my life. She showed me I was worth fighting for. But I still had to get up.

You are both the poison and the antidote. The same mind that spirals can also heal.

Rock bottom is a foundation, not a grave. Everything that breaks you can remake you if you choose to see it as solid ground to build on.

I got up off the mat. I learned a new trade. I learned a new skill. It gave me just enough leverage to get up. And that taught me something: sometimes you just need enough to get to the next step. You don't need to see the whole staircase. You just need to see the next step.

[YOUR TURN]

First: What was your "where we went to die" moment? When did you hit rock bottom? Tell the truth about how bad it got.

Second: How did you contribute to your own crisis? What role did you play? What choices did you make? What signs did you ignore?

Third: What did you do to get off the mat? How did you rebuild? Who showed up for you? And most importantly: What did you learn about yourself that you couldn't have learned any other way?

7

Dog-Eared

I was waiting in the lobby of a yoga studio, post-class, still in that slightly floaty headspace where your body feels loose and your mind is quiet. It was late 2012. I was standing by the window, waiting for a friend, half-paying attention to the people coming and going, when I saw it. On a small wooden table in the corner. Casual. Like it had been sitting there forever, waiting. HERLIFE Magazine. The cover caught my eye first, a beautiful woman, professional photography, clean design. A women's lifestyle publication. Glossy. Substantial. The kind of magazine that looked legitimate, professional, real. I picked it up. And the second I started flipping through the pages, something shifted inside me.

The photography was technically fine. Properly exposed. Decent composition. But it wasn't excellent. It wasn't the kind of photography that stopped you mid-scroll, that made you feel something, that elevated the subject into something more than what they were. The layouts were clean and organized.

Readable. Professional. But they could be sharper. More dynamic. More visual punch. The stories were interesting, profiles of local women doing cool things, fashion spreads, lifestyle features about wine country and local restaurants. But the images weren't supporting the content the way they should. They weren't amplifying the message. They weren't making you want to keep turning pages. The whole thing had incredible potential that wasn't being fully realized.

Standing there in that yoga studio lobby, flipping through page after page, I felt something I hadn't felt in years. Hunger. Not for food. For this. For the creative challenge of taking something good and making it better. For the scope of it, not just one client, one session, one moment frozen in time. But ongoing. Monthly. A platform. A voice. A way to reach thousands of people instead of dozens. For the first time since I'd started my photography business, I felt that pull toward something bigger. I thought: This needs help with photography. And then I thought: I could do this better. I tucked the magazine under my arm and took it home.

That night, I sat at my kitchen table with the magazine spread out in front of me. Rowdy was already in bed. Ronnie was watching TV. The house was quiet. And I started working. I dog-eared pages. I made notes in the margins with a pen, what I would change, what I would improve, what I would fix. I circled photos that needed better composition. I marked layouts that could be tighter, cleaner, more impactful. I wrote suggestions for story angles, for ways to make the content more compelling. I couldn't explain why I was so obsessed with it. I just knew it mattered.

There was something about this magazine, this tangible, physical thing that showed up every month and landed in people's hands, that felt important in a way digital never did. I'd spent years building an Instagram following, posting beautiful images online, watching likes and comments roll in. And it was fun. It was validating. But it was also ephemeral. Forgettable. Scrolled past in three seconds and gone. A magazine was different. A magazine sat on coffee tables. Got passed from friend to friend. Lived in doctor's offices and hair salons. Lasted. A magazine was legacy. And I wanted to be part of that.

The next morning, I called the number listed in the masthead. My heart was pounding as I dialed. The Voice was already spinning up its attack: Who do you think you are? They don't need your help. You're going to sound desperate and stupid. But I pushed through. The phone rang. And rang. And went to voicemail. I left a message. "Hi, my name is Dee Yates. I'm a photographer in Lodi, and I came across your magazine at a yoga studio. I think what you're doing is really great, and I have some ideas about how the photography could be even stronger. I'd love to talk if you're interested. Here's my number…" I hung up. And I waited.

Days went by. Then a week. Then two weeks. No one called me back. The Voice had a field day with that. See? They don't want your help. They don't need you. You're nobody to them. Let it go. But I couldn't let it go. I kept that magazine. Kept thinking about it. Kept adding more notes to the margins. Kept studying the layouts and the stories and the photography. I started looking for HERLIFE everywhere I went. Coffee shops. Bookstores. Anywhere that might carry it. I collected multiple issues. Dog-eared all of them. Filled them with notes and ideas and critiques.

Ronnie would see them spread out on the kitchen table and shake his head. "You're obsessed with that magazine." "I know," I'd say. "I can't explain it." But the truth was, I could explain it. I'd made a declaration when I was eighteen years old, standing in my mother's kitchen. Someday I'm going to own my own magazine. I'd forgotten I'd said it. The moment had disappeared from my conscious memory, buried under years of work and struggle and building and losing and rebuilding. But somewhere deep inside, that declaration was still alive. Still waiting. Still pulling me toward something I couldn't yet name.

Six months passed. Six months of keeping those dog-eared magazines, of studying them, of thinking about what I would do differently if I had the chance. And then my phone rang. "Hey, it's Katie." One of my studio clients. I'd photographed her wedding a few years back. I liked her. "Hey! How are you? It's been forever." "I'm good! Listen, I'm actually calling because I'm working for HERLIFE Magazine now. Selling advertising. And Kimberly, the owner, she's looking for a photographer." My heart stopped. "I immediately thought of you," Katie continued. "I showed her your work, and she loves it. She wants to meet you. Are you interested?" I didn't skip a beat. "Yes. Absolutely. When?" That's just how manifestation works perfectly.

Three days later, I was sitting across from Kimberly at House of Coffees in Lodi. She was exactly the kind of woman I wanted to learn from. Polished. Professional. Put-together in that effortless way that comes from actually knowing what you're doing, not faking it. She carried herself like someone who'd built something real. Who understood the weight and responsibility of running a business. Who took her work seriously. I liked her immediately. We became fast friends and are still best friends today.

We ordered coffee. Made small talk. And then I pulled out the magazine. The dog-eared one. The first one I'd picked up six months ago. The one with notes scribbled in every margin, pages folded over, entire sections marked with my thoughts and suggestions. I set it on the table between us. Kimberly's eyes went wide. "Is that…?" "One of your early issues," I said. "I've been studying it for six months. And I think I can help you make it better."

Then I walked her through everything. Page by page. Every photo I'd circled. Every layout I'd marked. Every suggestion I'd written. "This image would be stronger if you cropped it tighter here. See how the subject's face gets lost in all this negative space? If you brought the frame in closer, it would be more intimate. More powerful." "This spread would benefit from more white space. Right now it feels cramped. The eye doesn't know where to land." "This cover, the model's beautiful, but the styling isn't quite right. The colors are competing with each other instead of complementing. And the headline placement is blocking her face."

I wasn't gentle about it. I was direct. Specific. Honest. I

showed her exactly what I saw and exactly how I would fix it. She was floored at the balls I had in telling her what she was doing wrong in her magazine. But she also knew I was right.

When I finished, Kimberly was quiet for a moment. Then she said, "I want to work with you. On the spot. Right now." I blinked. "Really?" "I've been looking for someone who actually understands what I'm trying to build here. Someone who gets the vision. Someone who cares about making it excellent, not just good enough." She leaned forward. "Most people would have just sent me their portfolio and hoped I'd call. You spent six months studying my work. You did the homework. You came prepared with actual solutions. That tells me everything I need to know about how you work." She extended her hand. "When can you start?" I said, just give me a shot. Give me one chance. And she gave me that chance.

And just like that, I was part of HERLIFE Magazine. Starting in 2013, I began photographing stories for Kimberly. Fashion shoots. Profile features. Editorial spreads. Interior features. By then, my studio was truly thriving, the systems were dialed in, the high-end sales process was working, and sessions were profitable. But this was different. This was the bigger vision I'd been hungry for.

At first, I was just the photographer. But quickly, my role expanded. Kimberly saw how I approached the work, not just technically competent, but strategic. I understood how images served the story. How layouts directed the reader's eye. How design choices reinforced the brand. She began trusting me with more creative decisions. Art directing shoots.

Selecting photos. Working with designers on some of the featured layouts. By the next year, I was shooting her covers. And this went on for several years.

And Kimberly, brilliant, generous and incredibly talented Kimberly, let me watch everything. She didn't gate-keep. She didn't hide the business side from me. She treated me like a trusted partner, not just a contractor. She showed me how publishing actually worked. How to pitch advertisers. How to build relationships with local businesses. How to price ad space. How to negotiate printing contracts. How to manage distribution. She let me sit in on meetings with vendors. She walked me through P&L statements. She explained margins and overhead and what it actually cost to produce each issue. I was learning the entire business from someone who was brilliant at marketing, writing, editing and selling. And I soaked up everything.

I leveraged what I had. Sweat equity. I had a skill set. I gave it to Kimberly to make her business better and in exchange, she marketed my business, my photography business. And my photography business blew up. I was doing 25 to 30 weddings a year at anywhere from five to ten thousand dollars a wedding. I was also doing newborns anywhere from twenty-five hundred to five thousand dollars a session. I was doing portrait work the same. I was busy every single week.

I learned how to do sales. I learned how to negotiate contracts. I learned how to protect my images as assets. I learned how to sell those images as assets. I learned how to do in-person everything. Nothing was a digital throwaway. Everything was an in-person tangible product. I learned how to sell it like no one else was selling it. I became a master. I had mastery. I learned from masters and I set those things into motion. I worked hard to be the best. I wanted to be the best at what I did, not better than someone else. I stayed in my lane. Didn't look left, I didn't look right. I looked at my path, the path that was given to me, and I busted my ass on my own path.

While I was working with Kimberly, something else was happening too. I was being pulled back toward my roots. In 2015, I went to the Cowgirl Hall of Fame in Fort Worth, Texas for the first time with Sharon Camarillo, a legendary cowgirl and friend who'd become a mentor. Sharon had been inducted years earlier, and she attended every year as an honoree and she invited me to come celebrate with her.

Standing in that hall, surrounded by the history and legacy of Western women who'd broken barriers and built empires and refused to be told they couldn't do something, I felt something shift inside me. This was my heritage too. Not because I'd competed at their level. But because I came from this culture. From the Central Valley ranches and the rodeo grounds and the families who worked the land and raised cattle and lived by a code that valued grit over glamour.

I started going to the Cowgirl Hall of Fame every year after that. It became a pilgrimage. A reminder of where I came from and what I was capable of. By 2016, I'd started envisioning a book project, documenting the California cowgirls. The women who ran ranches, trained horses, competed in rodeos, kept the Western traditions alive. I started photographing them. Traveling to their ranches. Hearing their stories. Capturing their strength and grace and resilience. I was diving deep into that world, the culture I'd grown up around but had set aside while I built my photography business and worked in the more polished world of lifestyle magazines. I had no idea yet that this pull toward Western heritage would eventually lead me to a 58-year-old rodeo publication. That the skills I was learning from Kimberly would prepare me for something much bigger than a lifestyle magazine. But the seeds were being planted.

By 2016, I'd been working with Kimberly for about four years. I knew the magazine inside and out. I knew the readers. I knew the advertisers. I knew what stories worked and what fell flat. I knew which layouts got the most engagement and which covers sold the best. I knew how to pitch a story, how to art direct a shoot, how to work with subjects who were nervous in front of the camera. I knew the entire creative process from concept to execution. We built complete marketing campaigns for all types of businesses.

But I also knew the business side. I knew what it cost to print each issue. I knew the margins on advertising. I knew how subscription revenue worked. I knew the relationships with distributors and vendors. I'd learned every facet of the publishing business. Not from a textbook. Not from a degree program. From watching Kimberly do it month after month, year after year. From asking questions. From paying attention. From being present and engaged and genuinely curious about how it all worked. I'd been preparing for something without fully knowing what it was. And I was ready. I just didn't know it yet.

Looking back now, I can see that those years with Kimberly were the most important education I ever received. She was my mentor and she was more valuable than any college. More practical than any business course. Because I wasn't learning theory. I wasn't reading case studies. I wasn't taking tests. I was doing the actual work. Making real decisions. Seeing real consequences. I was learning how to run a magazine by being intimately involved in every aspect of running a magazine. And I was learning from someone who was excellent at it.

This is what I teach now in my online courses. Not theory. Not fluff. Not generic advice that sounds good but doesn't actually work. I teach the real stuff. The things you can only learn by doing. By being in the room. By watching someone who knows what they're doing and asking a thousand questions. I teach people how to get that kind of education without going to school. How to find mentors who will let you watch and learn. How to show up with value instead of just asking for opportunities. How to turn access into mastery.

Because here's the truth: The best education isn't in a classroom. It's in the field. It's working alongside someone who's already doing what you want to do. It's being trusted enough to see how the whole machine works. And then, when the time comes, being ready to run your own machine.

* * *

[THE LESSON]: Preparation Looks Like Obsession

You can't fake genuine interest. When I picked up that magazine, I wasn't strategizing or networking, I was fascinated. That authentic curiosity drove me to study it for six months before I ever met Kimberly. When you're pulled toward something, when you can't stop studying it, thinking about it, pay attention. That's not distraction. That's preparation.

The best mentors let you see everything. Kimberly didn't just hire me to take photos. She let me watch how she ran the entire operation. She treated me like someone capable of learning, not just executing tasks.

Sometimes the thing you're preparing for hasn't revealed itself yet. Trust that process. Preparation, even when you don't know what you're preparing for, is never wasted.

[YOUR TURN]

First: What are you obsessed with right now? What can't you stop thinking about, studying, wanting to understand? That might be your preparation showing you where to go next.

Second: Who has access to what you want to learn? What value can you bring them that would make them want to let you watch and learn?

Third: Where are you waiting for a title or official permission to start learning? What if you just started paying attention and showing up with value?

8

Pine Street

I stood in front of the little house on Pine Street in downtown Lodi with the keys in my hand. It was three years since I'd stood in an empty house with my baby on my hip and watched everything I'd built disappear. And now I was holding keys again. Not to a home this time. To a studio. A small house in the commercial district. Beautiful area. Historic neighborhood. The kind of place where people walked their dogs and stopped to look in shop windows and felt safe leaving their doors unlocked. The kind of place where having a business meant something. The landlord had just handed me the keys and driven away. And I was standing there alone, staring at this little house that was about to become mine. Not mine to own. Not yet. But mine to transform. Mine to bet on.

Nobody tells you about rebuilding after you lose everything: It's terrifying. Not the first time you take a risk. That first time, you're naive. You think: It'll work out. It has to work out. But the second time? After you've already failed? After you've already lost the house and had to start over? The second time, you know exactly what can go wrong. You know what it feels like to stand in an empty house and realize you have nothing left. You know what it feels like to rebuild credit point by point, month by month, proving to banks and landlords and everyone watching that you're not a risk anymore. You know what it feels like to live on leased ground, land you don't own, growing crops you might not get to harvest, never quite sure if you'll be there next year. So when you get another chance to bet on yourself, the fear is different. Not the naive fear of What if this doesn't work? But the bone-deep fear of What if I lose everything again?

I unlocked the door and stepped inside. The house was empty. Worn hardwood floors. Wallpaper peeling at the seams. Dated fixtures. Rooms that had been lived in and loved and then abandoned. But I could see past all of that. I could see the waiting room where clients would sit. The shooting space with professional lighting. The consultation area where I'd help people envision what their images could become. I could see my name on the door. My business cards on the counter. My work on the walls. I could see what it would become. And that vision, that ability to see potential where others saw work, that's what kept me moving forward.

For the next few weeks, I worked. Painting walls. Ripping up old carpet. Installing new flooring. Hanging lights. Building backdrops. My hands were blistered. My back ached. I'd come home exhausted, covered in paint and dust, barely able to move. That's the day my father came to see the space while I was in the middle of the rehab, and walked right back out.

Didn't say another word. Just left.

I sat there on the floor, hammer in hand, watching him drive away. In that moment, the weight of his doubt pressed down on me. I knew what he was thinking: You just lost everything. Why are you risking it again? But I also knew what he'd taught me, even if he didn't say it out loud: When someone knocks you down, you ball up your fist and you don't stop swinging until you're back on your feet. That's what this was. Getting back on my feet. So I kept working. Because this wasn't just a studio. This was proof. Proof that I could rebuild. Proof that failure didn't define me. Proof that losing everything once didn't mean I couldn't build it back better. Proof that I belonged. I thought about all the years I'd been shooting out of my home. Weddings and Family portraits for cheap. Newborn sessions where I'd move furniture around in my living room and hope the client didn't notice we were in a house, not a studio. Making it work. Making money. But never quite feeling legitimate. Always feeling like I was one step away from someone asking: Who do you think you are?

But a brick-and-mortar studio? That changed everything. When you have a physical location, when clients can walk into a space with your name on it, with professional equipment and a waiting room and artwork on the walls, you become something different. You become real. Official. Legitimate. Not just "a photographer who works from home." But a business owner. A professional. Someone worth paying for. I knew this from my real estate days. Perception creates value. It's not just about being good at what you do. It's about presenting yourself in a way that communicates: This is professional. This is worth paying for. This is not negotiable. When clients walked into my studio, they knew, before I even took a single photo, that this was going to cost more than the photographer down the street. And they were okay with that. Because the environment matched the price. The experience matched the investment. This is what mastery looks like: knowing that the work matters, but the presentation matters just as much.

The day I opened, I stood outside and looked at the sign I'd hung above the door. Simple. Clean. Professional. My name. My business. And I thought about how far I'd come. From the $600 Costco camera my parents had sacrificed to buy me. From shooting weddings for free just to build a portfolio. From the leased ground where we learned to survive. From every person who doubted me, every moment I doubted myself, every time The Voice said people like you don't get to do this. And here I was. Doing it.

I stopped giving away digital files. This was a big shift, and it wasn't easy at first. A lot of photographers were moving toward digital-only packages, shoot the session, hand over a USB drive, done. Quick, easy, profitable. But I saw something they didn't. When you give someone digital files, you're giving them homework. They have to figure out what to do with those images. They have to decide which ones to print, where to print them, how to frame them, where to hang them. And most people never do it. So those beautiful images, the ones they paid for, the ones that captured their family or their baby or their life at that exact moment, they sit on a hard drive somewhere. Maybe they post a few to Facebook. Maybe they get printed at Costco and stuck in a drawer. But they don't become heirlooms.

I wanted to create heirlooms. So I built a complete system, one that would eventually become the model I teach in all my photography courses. A system that transformed how I worked, what I charged, and how clients experienced photography. I learned how to do sales. I learned how to negotiate contracts. I learned how to protect my images as assets. I learned how to sell those images as assets. I learned how to do in-person everything. Nothing was a digital throwaway. Everything was an in-person tangible product. I learned how to sell it like no one else was selling it. I became a master. I had mastery. I learned from masters and I set those things into motion.

Before we even scheduled the shoot, I brought the client in for a consultation. Not a quick phone call. A real, in-person meeting. We'd sit down with coffee. I'd ask questions. "What are you envisioning for these images?" "Where do you see them in your home?" "Is this for you, or are you thinking about gifts for family?" "What rooms are we decorating? What's your style, modern, traditional, rustic?" "What matters most to you about this session?" I'd show them my portfolio. Not on a screen, actual printed albums, framed wall art, finished products they could touch and feel.

I'd walk them through examples: "See this family? They wanted something for their living room. We did a large canvas above the fireplace. It became the focal point of the whole space." "This client wanted a gallery wall in her hallway. We created a collection of five images that told the story of her kids at this age. Every time she walks past it, she feels it." And then I'd set expectations. Very clearly. Very directly. "Here's how this works. We're not just doing a photo session. We're creating art for your walls. After the shoot, you'll come back for a sales meeting. We'll go through the images together, and I'll help you see what's possible. We'll design the pieces, choose the frames, plan the installation. This is a complete experience."

By the time they left that consultation, they saw all of my pricing on products and services so there would never be any sticker-shock. They understood: This isn't $300 and a USB drive. This is an investment in family heirlooms. And if they weren't ready for that? We didn't book the session. I only worked with clients who valued what I was creating and wanted to spend time with me.

When I showed up to shoot, I wasn't just capturing moments anymore. I was creating products. Every image I took, I was thinking: Would this look beautiful as a 30x40 canvas? Would this work in a gallery wall? Is this something they'll want to see every day for the next twenty years? I shot with intention. With an eye for how these images would live in their home. And I shot generously, giving them options, variety, moments they didn't even know they wanted until they saw them.

But I also kept control of the process. I didn't hand over hundreds of unedited images and let them choose. I curated. I edited. I selected the best work and presented it in a way that told a story. Because here's what I learned: clients don't actually want to make all the decisions. They want to be guided. They want someone who knows what they're doing to say, "Here's what's going to look incredible in your home."

A week or two after the shoot, the client came back to the studio. Required. Non-negotiable. I'd have everything ready, images printed as proofs, displayed around the room, carefully arranged. We'd sit down together, and I'd walk them through their images. But I wasn't just showing them photos. I was helping them see their future. "Look at this one. Can you see it above your fireplace? A 40x60 canvas in a walnut float frame. It would anchor your entire living room. Every time you walk in, you'd see your family, right there, at the heart of your home." "These three images, look how they work together. They tell a story. We could do a triptych for your hallway. You'd walk past them every day, and instead of blank walls, you'd see these moments. Your kids at this exact age. This exact time in your life." "This is the one for the grandparents. This is the one that's going to make them cry when they open it. We'll do a custom album, thick pages, museum-quality printing, bound in leather. It's not just a photo album. It's a family heirloom."

I wasn't selling photos. I was selling emotion. Memory. Legacy. And I didn't just take their order and send them home with a receipt. I offered to come to their house and install everything myself. I'd show up with a level, a tape measure, and an eye for what worked. I'd help them figure out spacing, height, arrangement. I'd put the holes in the walls, hang the frames, make sure everything was perfect. Because here's the thing most people don't realize: clients are nervous about hanging expensive art. They don't know if they're doing it right. They're afraid of messing up their walls. So I did it for them.

And when we were done, when they stood back and saw their images, their family, their babies, their story, beautifully displayed in their home exactly where it belonged? They got it. They understood why this wasn't $500. Because it wasn't just photos. It was transformation. It was art that changed how they felt in their own home. It was something their grandchildren would look at someday and say, "Tell me about this."

It took me about a year to refine everything until it was smooth. The system generated multiple six figures annually. And clients, they were happy to pay it. Not because I was the best photographer in town, though I'd put in my 10,000 hours and I was damn good. But because I'd built a complete system that made the experience worth the investment. Customer service came first. I answered emails within 24 hours. I showed up on time, early, always. I listened to what clients wanted. I made them feel special, valued, taken care of every step of the way. When they reached out, I responded. When they had questions, I answered. When they needed help, I showed up. That level of service created trust. And trust made everything else possible.

Quality backed it up. Every image was edited beautifully. Every print was museum-quality. Every frame was chosen carefully to complement their style and their home. I didn't cut corners. I didn't settle for "good enough." I delivered work I was genuinely proud of. Work that would last. Work that would be treasured. And they got me every step of the way. From the first consultation to the final installation, I was with them. I guided them. I made it easy. I didn't make them figure it out on their own. I didn't hand them homework. I didn't leave them hanging. I walked them through the entire journey, and when it was done, they had something beautiful that they didn't have to think about again, it was just there, in their home, part of their daily life. That's what people pay for. Not just the product. The entire experience.

I targeted middle to upper-income women. Mothers who wanted beautiful portraits of their babies. Families who were updating their homes and wanted art that meant something. Women who valued quality and were willing to invest in things that mattered. I marketed directly to them. I showed up where they were, boutique shops, high-end neighborhoods, community events. I built relationships with interior designers and real estate agents who worked with the same clientele. And word spread. "You have to use Dee. She's incredible." "It's expensive, but it's worth every penny." "She came to my house and hung everything. It looks like a magazine." My calendar filled up. I was booking months in advance. I was running a successful, profitable business, one that I'd built from the ground up, with systems I'd designed myself. And it wasn't luck. It wasn't a fluke. It was mastery.

I worked hard to be the best. I'd put in my 10,000 hours behind the camera. I'd learned from the best photographers I could find, I'd studied sales at that portrait studio, watching them close deal after deal with a system that worked. I'd learned contracts and negotiations from John in Stockton during my real estate years. And now I was putting it all together in a way that actually worked.

During these years, I was also shooting for HERLIFE Magazine. Kimberly and I started working together because she saw what I was building. She saw the quality of my work. She saw that I understood how to create images that told stories, that connected with people, that elevated a brand. My studio success gave me credibility. It proved I wasn't just talented, I was professional. I could deliver. I could run a business. And that credibility opened doors. The skills I was developing in the studio, how to art direct, how to create compelling visual stories, how to work with subjects, how to think about images in context, those skills translated directly to editorial work. I was learning two sides of the same business. And both were preparing me for something bigger.

My photography business was doing gangbusters because I was marketing in the women's magazine. That was part of our trade. I leveraged what I had. Sweat equity. And it helped my photography business blow up. I was busy every single week.

In 2017, I bought the photography studio property outright. The little house on Pine Street in downtown Lodi that I'd been renting for four years, I purchased it. It was mine. Not rented. Not leased. Mine. Six years after losing everything in foreclosure, I owned two properties. The ranch. The studio. Concrete, undeniable proof that I'd climbed back up.

That moment meant more than I can explain. It wasn't just a business decision. It was vindication. It was evidence that everything I'd been building, the systems, the reputation, the hard work, it all mattered. It all counted. By 2018, I'd turn that studio into an Airbnb. That studio was the foundation of everything I was building. It proved to me, and to everyone watching, that I could take an idea, a vision, a dream, and turn it into a thriving business. It proved that mastery gives value education cannot. It proved that you don't need permission to build something real. You just need skill, systems, and the courage to bet on yourself. Even when you're terrified. Even when everyone doubts you. Even when The Voice says you're going to fail again.

The Voice was quieter during those years. Not gone, never gone. But quieter. Because every time a client paid for a session, every time someone cried when they saw their images, every time I installed art in someone's home and they hugged me and said "thank you for making this so easy," The Voice had less ammunition. You're not qualified. But I had a business that said otherwise. You can't make money taking pictures. But my bank account said otherwise. Who do you think you are? And I was starting to have an answer: I'm someone who showed up. Someone who did the work. Someone who built something from nothing and made it successful. I'm someone who writes her own damn story... and I ain't asking for permission

* * *

[THE LESSON]: Customer Service First, Quality Second, Sales Third

Most people get the order wrong. They create a product, then figure out sales, then worry about service later. But that's backward.

Customer service comes first. Answer emails promptly, show up on time, make people feel valued. People forgive imperfect products if the experience is good, but won't forgive bad service.

Quality comes second. Once you serve people well, focus on making your product excellent. Never stop learning. Don't cut corners. Deliver work you're proud of.

Sales comes third. When you genuinely believe in what you're selling, when you've already taken care of people and delivered quality, sales becomes easy. Because you're not selling. You're serving.

Take care of people. Create something excellent. Help them see the value. That's the whole game.

[YOUR TURN]

First: How do you currently treat your customers or clients? Where are you excelling? Where could you improve?

____

____

____

____

____

Second: What would "heirloom quality" look like in your business? How could you elevate what you're offering from "good enough" to "exceptional"?

____

____

____

____

____

Third: What systems do you need to build? What would a complete system look like, one that guides clients through the entire experience and makes it easy for them to say yes?

9

Paint on the Canvas

The only way to start a project that is in your heart, that you're passionate about, is by starting. Just start. One step in front of the other in front of the other in front of the other. This is something I have mastered, and the only way I've mastered it is by doing it, by being a creative being that has lots of ideas and that spends time writing those ideas down and building them into something instead of just shelving them and letting them die. The most important thing we can do is breathe life into the ideas that we have.

In 2016, I had an idea for a book.

I had been a photographer since the year 2000, and I wanted to take beautiful photos of cowgirls and tell their stories in pictures. David Stoecklein, who was a world-famous Western photographer, was someone that I looked up to and that I watched his work for years and years. I always wanted to be like him. And at some point, I realized that the only way to become like him is to start doing the work.

But the question that runs through most of our minds is, how do I do that? And what gives me the authority to do that? And who do you think you are?

Well, the only roadblocks you really have are the ones in your own mind. You have to believe you're capable and then you have to take steps in order to make those ideas and dreams become something. See, if you have the idea, you have to put it on paper and then you have to develop the steps to manifest it, to bring it into fruition. This is how I've learned to organize my thoughts and my ideas.

It started with a photograph. A black and white image of Dale Evans, my mother's godmother, dressed in Western wear, confident and beautiful, frozen in time. Roy Rogers and Dale Evans were my mother's godparents. She grew up on their ranch. My grandpa was Roy Rogers' ranch manager. I'd seen that photo of Dale Evans a hundred times growing up. Hanging in my mother's house. Tucked into old albums. A piece of family history I'd never thought much about.

But one day, I looked at it differently. She had the cutest skirt on, and the cutest little cowgirl hat, embroidered top and the scarf and the little boots. Everything had such a feel to it, a time frame, an era. And I thought, oh my gosh, that is such a moment in time that has expired, and here we are celebrating it. We should be doing the same thing right now in this era. Documenting the women, the clothes, the tack, the scenery, the style of horses, the style of equipment, what the kids were wearing, what they were doing, and celebrating them.

I saw more than just Dale Evans. I saw a moment preserved. A culture documented. A woman's story told through image. And I thought: Who's doing this now? Who's photographing the cowgirls of today, the real ones, not the Instagram versions, and preserving their stories before they're lost? Who's stopping time to celebrate the women holding ranches together, keeping traditions alive, doing the unglamorous work that sustains Western culture?

Nobody. So I decided: I would.

This grandiose idea I had was to memorialize all these cowgirls. But how the heck was I going to do that? How was I going to get my hands around all the different cultures that are micro-cultures within the cowgirl culture? Cowgirls in Northern Nevada wear completely different clothes and use completely different tack than somebody in West Texas, in contrast to someone in northern Louisiana, in contrast to someone in Montana, or North Dakota, or Illinois, or South Carolina.

The way I could get my hands around it was to break it down into pieces and start thinking about the little micro-cultures within cowgirl culture in America. Holy shit, where do I start? So you develop better problem-solving skills. I want to photograph cowgirls. Cool. What cowgirls? I don't know, the cowgirls that are cool. How can I divide this up to make it digestible? Every region, every area, every state has its own style. I can divide this up into states.

California. I'll start in California. California is where cowboys were invented. Nobody wants to say that anymore as history is being forgotten. Texas tries to take full credit for cowboys. Well, California is where cowboys got started. And I'm going to celebrate the cowgirls of California.

    -No offense Texans!

Now at this time I had a family and a new ranch and a business and responsibilities. How was I going to make this project work between family, work, my kid's school, sports, clients, the animals on the ranch and that responsibility I had? How was I going to do that?

Well, I could start with my own backyard. So I took a goal and I broke it down into small bites so that I could easily get my hands around it. There's always a way to figure out your dreams and figure out creative projects.

I met with a woman named Sharon Camarillo. A woman who's been in the industry for decades and knows everyone worth knowing. My sister used to house-sit for her, and Sharon used to come to the feed store where I worked as a young girl. I asked her for a lunch date at the Dancing Fox restaurant in Lodi, California.

She met me, and she was a very busy lady, so I made sure to get right down to the point. She came in hot and fast (and, of course, well dressed) and said, "Okay, what can I do for you?"

Saddle up because opportunity is knocking. Are you brave enough and smart enough to see that opportunity is there?

Yes, I am.

"Okay, I have this idea," I told her. "I want to do a book. I want to tell stories about real cowgirls and memorialize the era that we're in right now. I want to feature amazing cowgirls in California. I want to feature their style. I want to feature their clothes, their tack, their body language, the horses that they ride. I want to show everything that they've got to show."

"Cool. How can I help?"

"I need a list of women. I need a list of women to get started. Ten would be great."

Sharon, Cowgirl Hall of Famer, gave me ten. Amazing women, many of them in the Cowgirl Hall of Fame with her. She gave me phone numbers for all ten of these women and she sent me on my merry way. I told her what I had in mind, this would be a photography book, a coffee table book, rich in photos and some stories and thoughts and ideas and poems that I had while I was on the road memorializing fashion and culture and California in this book specifically.

I decided to map out areas of California, areas that I could get to under eight hours in my own car, and places I could get to photograph several different ranches from Thursday to Sunday. I knew I could get help with my son from my mom and dad, and then my son would have time at home with Ronnie who would be home for the weekend. Ronnie would be taking care of them, so this allowed me to just schedule my weekends and go out and photograph these unbelievable ideas I had.

I took a map of California and I penciled in the ten women that I had and I put markers on the map. I started getting a hold of them on Facebook or through phone numbers, and I asked them if they'd be interested. I picked women in a specific weekend that lived near each other so I would take anywhere from two to five, maybe six, and I'd ask them if they were available. I told them my idea.

These women had to be so trusting because they didn't know me, and I had never shot one of these projects before. They were really going out on a limb by saying yes to me. I would send them to my website, my photography website, so they knew that I was a professional. I would organize them accordingly and go out and shoot them.

I got the idea on paper. I got a few references. I reached out to them without fear, and I organized what I was going to do and I stayed on track. One after the other after the other, women were saying yes to me. In those first ten, every time I went out to photograph a woman, I asked her for another ten women. Pretty soon I had a list that was far and wide.

When I was on my travels, there would be times where there were impromptu women that weren't necessarily on my list, but I said yes to them and they said yes to me and we would do shoots. And these shoots were unbelievable.

So I hit the road. I had my little four-door sedan and my first stop. I was so nervous. I pulled into this big reined cow horse ranch in San Ynez, California. There were some pretty famous trainers there, and they were all out working. I stepped out of my car with my backpack on, my camera equipment inside, and I was so nervous.

My first cowgirl that I photographed was so kind and so generous. She took me around all of her handmade tack, much of it she built and made herself. I felt so nervous and so scared and so elementary, as if I had started a whole new career and that I had never been shooting before. But I already knew how to do this, and I had to remind myself: You can do this. No one else is going to do this. You can do this. Period.

What I've learned repeatedly is that most people are too scared to jump. They're too afraid to set their dreams on fire and go after them. Period. They're not willing to do the work it takes. The work. The work of being gone every weekend. The work of sitting up all night editing. And the work that you know is difficult and challenging and scary and fearful, but you saddle up and you do it anyway.

I've noticed this across every business I've ever started or done. You have to go the extra mile. The extra work. The extra late nights. The extra money that you have to save. The extra strategy or workaround to make things fit or move or think things all the way through or figure out a way to fix it or build it or create it. It takes creativity and it takes resourcefulness and it takes grit and determination. You have to be able to go and try and push even through the things you don't think you can do.

So I did it. From one ranch to the next ranch to the next ranch, I photographed these women. Every time I pulled into a ranch,

I didn't know where I was going or what I was going to see or what was going to happen. And that was exhilarating.

On the road, I got to listen to the music that inspired me. And the most amazing thing happened that I learned about myself, and that was that creativity would download in these moments of being alone with myself, on the road, in my car, listening to music that moved me and moved my heart.

I would end up writing in my journal. It would be sitting next to me in the seat on my right, and I would just have a pen and paper and it would be so messy. But I would write, write, write, write, write, write, write. Because all these feelings and thoughts about who I am and what I wanted to be and the inspiration that was brought to me by other women and the heartfelt things that I was learning about people and history and creativity would all start pouring out of me.

On Thursday afternoons, after I mapped out my cowgirls, I would take off and go and photograph anywhere from two to maybe six different women in different locations. This started adding up until I got to fifty different women.

Photograph the first girl. Look at the photos. Do the next one. Do the next one. Do the next one. Put them on paper. Put another paper down. Put another paper down. Now you have two hundred fifty papers. Now organize them. Now write about it. Now bind it in a book. Now get the legalities around your copyright. Order your ISBN. Design the cover. Have it copy edited. Have it copy edited again. Confirm that all the sizing's right. Look at it again. Press print. You have a book!

Start somewhere. Photograph the first girl.

Here are some other things that I've learned. Creative work isn't a mathematical problem. Therefore, it will never be perfect. I cannot tell you how many times I've worked with women in their businesses who want their creation to be perfect before they show the world. Bullshit. I'm here to call bullshit. I'm here to tell you that's avoidance behavior. I've been guilty of it. I recognize it very well. You're avoiding because you're scared. What are you scared of? Rejection. Why? Because you'll starve to death if the tribe doesn't accept you.

Who cares? Who f*king cares?

Creative work isn't a mathematical problem, therefore it will never be perfect. So stop trying to make it perfect. Press send.

Creatives that are successful are people that can create in the right side of the brain and also have the balls to press send when it's ready to go. Have the balls to press send when it's time to show the world. Most people have one or the other. Most people that have the business sense to pull the trigger, lack the creative ability to make things: and what and vice versa. Those that are successful, have or can do both.

Just start. Start somewhere. Stop making excuses as to why you can't start. Just start somewhere. Get some paint on the canvas.

* * *

[THE LESSON]: Get Paint on the Canvas

The only way to breathe life into your ideas is to start. Not when you're ready. Not when it's perfect. Not when you have all the answers. Now.

Most people never finish their dreams because they're waiting for perfection. They want their creation to be perfect before they show the world. That's avoidance behavior. That's fear dressed up as standards. You're avoiding because you're scared of rejection, scared that the tribe won't accept you.

Here's what I learned on the road photographing fifty cowgirls: You don't need permission. You don't need to know how it ends. You just need to start.

Break big dreams into small bites. I couldn't photograph every cowgirl in America. But I could photograph ten in California. Then I could ask each one for ten more names. Then I could map out weekend trips under eight hours from home. Then I could photograph two to six women per trip. One step in front of the other in front of the other.

Creative work isn't a mathematical problem, therefore it will never be perfect. Stop waiting for perfect. Press send. Get paint on the canvas.

The creatives who succeed are the ones who can create and

also have the balls to show the world. You need both. Start somewhere. Start ugly. Start scared. Just start.

[YOUR TURN]

First: What idea have you been holding in your heart that you haven't started? What dream have you been shelving instead of building? Write it down. Breathe life into it right now.

____

____

____

____

____

Second: How can you break that big dream into small bites? What's the smallest first step you could take this week? Who could give you your first list of ten? Map it out.

____

____

Third: What are you waiting to perfect before you show the world? Where is perfectionism actually avoidance behavior? What would it look like to press send anyway?

---

* * *

10

Sell it To Me

We were sitting on Kimberly's couch in her house in Folsom, coffee mugs on the table between us, planning the next year for HERLIFE Magazine. This was how we always did it. Comfortable. Collaborative. Two friends who'd spent about four years creating together, talking through what stories we wanted to tell, which advertisers and we needed to nurture, what the editorial calendar should look like. It was 2016. Her little babies were running around the living room, toys scattered on the floor, that beautiful chaos of young motherhood that I remembered from when Rowdy was small. She had just had her third child. The house smelled like coffee and baby lotion and the faint vanilla of whatever candle she had burning in the kitchen.

I had my notebook open, I was jotting down story ideas, potential cover subjects, photo concepts that would work with the themes we were discussing. This was the work I loved. The creative planning. The "what if we did this?" conversations. The way Kimberly's eyes would light up when we landed on something good.

And then she said it. "My husband got a job in Boston."

I looked up from my notebook. "Oh wow. Congratulations. That's a big move." She nodded. Took a breath. "I'm selling the magazine. I have to sell the company."

Time stopped. I could hear everything with unnatural clarity. The kids playing. The hum of the refrigerator in the kitchen. My own heartbeat. Selling the magazine. The magazine I'd been studying for six months before I ever met her. The magazine I'd dog-eared and marked up and dreamed about. The magazine I'd worked on for almost four years, shooting covers and features, consulting on layouts and content, learning every single piece of how it all worked. The magazine that, if I was being honest with myself, I'd been preparing to own since I was eighteen years old and made that declaration in my mother's kitchen.

The Voice started immediately. Don't say anything stupid. She probably already has buyers lined up. People with more money. More experience. More everything. You can't afford this. You don't know how to run a magazine. You're just the photographer. But underneath The Voice, there was something else. Something quieter but stronger. A knowing. This opportunity was always meant to be mine.

And that is when I had the split-second moment to stop being afraid and to ask for what I wanted.

I remember feeling all this emotion welling up and my tongue got stiff and my mouth got tight and I almost missed the opportunity that changed my life forever. Inside, you go through all this powerful self-talk and shame about being good enough, being smart enough, being qualified enough, knowing enough. Rejection. All these things in a split second.

But in that split second, I was like, f*k it. What do I have to lose? What's the worst that can happen? She says no. And honestly, If I'm not brave enough to ask for what I want then I should just pack it up and go home now.

I didn't think about it. Didn't analyze it. Didn't make a pros and cons list in my head. My mouth opened, and four words came out: "Sell it to me."

Kimberly blinked. Sat back slightly on the couch. Looked at me like she was trying to figure out if I was serious. "Are you serious?"

"Dead serious."

Here's what happened in my body in that moment: My hands went cold. My heart was pounding so hard I could feel it in my throat. I could hear The Voice screaming now, a full-volume assault: What are you doing? You can't afford this. You don't know what you're doing. You're going to embarrass yourself. Take it back. Say you were kidding.

But I didn't take it back. I stood tall, chin up, eyes forward. I held Kimberly's eyes and said it again. "I want to buy it. I know you probably have other people interested. I know I might not have as much money as some of them. But I know this magazine. I understand what you've built. And I will take care of it."

She was quiet for a long moment. Then she said, "It's a lot. Running this business. It's not just the creative side. There's the operations, the finances, the sales, managing the team, dealing with printers and distributors and advertisers who pay late or want to renegotiate. It's a beast."

"I know," I said. "I've been watching you do it for four years. I've learned from the best."

She looked right back at me. "It's a beast. Are you sure that you want that?"

And I searched myself for a second and I looked back at her and I said, "Abso-fucking-lutely. Yes, I know it's a beast and I want it."

She smiled at that. A small smile, but genuine. "Let me think about it," she said. "There are other people who've expressed interest. I need to talk to my husband. I need to figure out the logistics."

"Okay," I said. "But I'm serious. And I'm not going anywhere."

I drove home from that meeting with my hands shaking on the steering wheel. What had I just done? I'd committed, out loud, to Kimberly, to buying a magazine I had no idea how to pay for. I didn't have a business loan lined up. I didn't have investors waiting in the wings. What I had was savings from the photography studio, credit I'd rebuilt slowly and painfully after the foreclosure, equity in the ranch we'd bought in 2015, and a certainty that this was mine to do. But certainty doesn't pay for a successful magazine business. So I had to figure out the money. And I had to compete.

Over the next several months, I became what I would later describe as "a dog on a bone." There were other buyers. Female buyers. Serious buyers. One of them I knew. She had way more experience than I did. More money. More credentials. More everything. And she was competing hard.

The Voice had an absolute field day during those months. She's going to beat you. Look at her resume. Look at her connections. Look at her bank account. You're a photographer from Lockeford. She's a serious businesswoman. Kimberly's going to choose her. Of course she's going to choose her. Why would she pick you? You're going to lose this. And everyone's going to know you tried and failed. You're embarrassing yourself. Just back out now before it gets worse.

But I didn't back out. I spent every day with Kimberly, and I wouldn't let it go. I wanted to know everything she knew. Even if she didn't pick me, I was showing her that I wanted it more. And so I began learning right then and there. What can we do today? What can I learn today? What are you doing today? Can I watch you? Can I shadow you?

I called Kimberly. I texted her. I showed up at the magazine office. I made it clear, every single day, that I wanted this more than anyone else. I wasn't pushy. I wasn't aggressive. I was just present. Persistent. Unavoidable. When she mentioned she had a meeting with another potential buyer, I asked if I could send her a written proposal outlining my vision for the magazine. When she said she was worried about the transition being smooth for the team, I reminded her that I already knew everyone, that I'd been working alongside them for years. When she expressed concern about whether I could handle the financial side, I showed her my photography studio numbers, the systems I'd built, the revenue I was generating, the proof that I knew how to run a profitable business.

I wasn't just saying I wanted it. I was showing her why I was the right person to have it. And I was willing to outwork everyone else. That's when I began telling her how capable I am and why I would be the best choice. I put into motion all of the confidence that I had, every ounce of it that I had inside of me, I put into motion.

The other buyers? They were qualified. They were experienced. They had the credentials. But I had something they didn't: I knew this magazine inside and out. I'd been living it, breathing it for four years. And I wanted it more. I was willing to do whatever it took. Work longer. Fight harder. Prove myself over and over again. Because this wasn't just a business opportunity. This was my declaration from eighteen years old finally coming true. This was everything I'd been preparing for my entire life.

Meanwhile, I was having other conversations. Conversations

with Ronnie about what this would mean for our family, for our finances, for our future. Conversations with my banker about loans and equity and what we could leverage. Conversations with myself, late at night, lying awake, running the numbers over and over, about whether this was brilliant or insane. When I told my father, his response was predictable. He told me I was crazy. Asked if I'd really thought this through. Warned me about all the ways it could fail. The familiar pattern of doubt. But I'd learned by then to move forward anyway.

And because of that tenacity and that fire and that drive and that sweat equity of doing things for her for free, she looked at me after a couple months of this and said, "It's you. I'm going to sell it to you because I know how much you want this. I've talked to all the buyers," she said. "And I've made my decision."

"I want to sell it to you."

I sat down. Actually sat down on the floor of my studio, phone pressed to my ear, because my legs wouldn't hold me anymore. "Really?"

"Really. You've shown me how much you want this. You understand what I've built here. You care about the readers, the advertisers, the team. You've been relentless, in the best way. You didn't just tell me you wanted it. You showed me. Over and over again." She paused. "And honestly? I trust you. I know you'll take care of it. The other buyers were qualified, but you… you love this magazine. I can see it. And that matters more than anything else."

I was crying. "Thank you. I promise I won't let you down."

"I know you won't," she said. And I could hear the smile in her voice. "Now let's figure out how to make this happen."

Here's what "figuring out how to make this happen" actually looked like: I leveraged everything. I leveraged one asset to the next asset to the next asset. The savings I'd built from the photography studio over five years? That became part of the down payment. The credit I'd rebuilt slowly, paying every bill on time for years, proving I was responsible? That became access to a business loan. The equity we'd built in our ranch, the one we'd bought in 2015, the one we'd worked so hard to own after losing everything? I leveraged that too. I leveraged sweat equity to begin to build a farm at a rental, to buy my next farm that I owned, to continue building my business, to continue building a studio, to buying the magazine. I'm building assets and I'm leveraging the first asset to buy the next asset to buy the next asset to buy the next asset. I used very little. I mean the minimum you could possibly have.

Everything we'd built. Everything we'd worked for. Not because I was reckless. Not because I didn't understand the risk. But because I knew, bone-deep, soul-certain, that this was mine to do. And betting on myself was the best play I had. When you know something like that, you don't hesitate. You don't wait for a safer option. You don't play small. You go all in.

The transition took several months. Kimberly walked me through everything, contracts, vendor relationships, advertiser expectations, distribution logistics, the financial side of running a publication. She introduced me to everyone as the new owner. She handed over the passwords, the files, the contacts, the institutional knowledge that can't be written down. By the end of that summer, we had closed a deal and she was in full training mode with me. And then, in mid 2017, it was mine. HERLIFE Magazine. The magazine I'd studied in a yoga studio lobby five years earlier. The magazine I'd dog-eared and marked up and dreamed about. The magazine I'd worked on for four years, learning everything I could. The magazine I'd fought for, competed for, refused to give up on. Mine.

Here's what nobody tells you about achieving a dream you've held since childhood: It's terrifying. The moment you get the thing you've wanted your whole life, The Voice shifts tactics. It's not "you can't have this" anymore. It's "now that you have it, you're going to lose it. You're going to fail. Everyone's watching. Everyone's waiting to see if you can actually do this. What if you can't? What if you prove them all right, that you were never qualified for this in the first place?" But I'd learned something by then. The Voice never goes away. It just changes its argument. And you don't silence it by achieving more or proving yourself or finally being "enough." You silence it by doing the work anyway.

And it was a whirlwind from there on out because I had to learn a lot of new skill sets. I had to meet a lot of clients. I had a lot of pressure, pressure I'd never felt before. It taught me how to deal with pressure. It taught me how to deal with clients with bigger expecations. It taught me about deeper, tighter timelines. It taught me about writing.

This is where I started writing. I began writing my publisher's note, the welcome into the magazine. That's where I became in touch with my writing skills. I had to look at all my shame around being able to write. And find my confidence and build my confidence around that. Just put paint on the canvas, girl. Start. Just start. Just get started. Start writing.

And I did. I wrote. And I had an amazing editor at the time named Marilyn. I told her, "Marilyn, I don't know how to write. I'm not a good writer. I don't understand the parameters around technical writing." And I remember her saying this and it was a very pivotal moment for me. She said, "It doesn't matter if you're a good technical writer. You have something to say. Having something to say is more important than being a technical writer. Put your thoughts on paper and I'll help you with the technicalities."

I ran HERLIFE Magazine for years. Years of making mistakes and fixing them. Of building relationships with advertisers and readers and the team. Of creating content I was proud of. Of proving, month after month, issue after issue, that I could do this. I learned how to manage P&L's. How to negotiate with printers. How to handle late-paying advertisers. How to keep a team motivated. How to pivot when something wasn't working. I learned how to run a media business. Not from a business school. Not from a textbook. From doing it. From leveraging everything and jumping in with both feet and figuring it out as I went.

Understand this, I was the girl who failed English. Multiple times. The girl who couldn't write a proper essay to save her life in high school. And I became the publisher and editor-in-chief of a magazine. I learned editorial. Layout design. Content strategy. Brand voice. Storytelling. The same girl who failed English in high school. None of this was taught in the community college photography classes I took. None of this came from a textbook or a degree program. I learned it by doing it. By saying yes before I was ready. By betting on myself. By going all in.

I this knowledge is what I offer in my Magazine Mastery course. The real stuff. The things you can only learn by building a business from the ground up. By making mistakes and fixing them. By taking risks that terrify you and coming out the other side. I teach people how to do what I did: Write their own damn story. Because here's the truth most people won't tell you: You don't need permission. You don't need credentials. You don't need someone to hand you an opportunity. You just need to show up and say: "I want this. And I'm willing to do whatever it takes to make it happen." And then you have to prove it. Over and over again. Until they can't say no.

Looking back now, I can see that buying HERLIFE was never actually about the magazine itself. It was about proving, to myself, to The Voice, to everyone who'd ever doubted me, that the girl who failed English could build something extraordinary. It was about rewriting the story I'd been told about who I was and what I was capable of. It was about stepping into a room where I didn't "belong" and claiming my seat at the table anyway. Because that's what writing your own story actually means. It means rejecting the narrative other people have written for you. It means taking the opportunities that terrify you. It means leveraging everything you've built and jumping in with both feet and figuring it out as you go. It means being willing to outwork everyone else who wants what you want. It means becoming the person you always knew you could be, even when everyone else thought you were crazy. And it means teaching other people how to do the same thing. Because if I can do it, then you can too. You absolutely can.

* * *

[THE LESSON]: The Split-Second Decision

Big life changes don't require months of planning. The biggest decisions happen in split seconds. "Sell it to me." Three words. Two seconds. But those words changed everything.

Here's the truth: split-second decisions aren't actually split-second. When Kimberly told me she was selling, I didn't pull that answer out of thin air. I'd been preparing for that moment my entire life. Studying fashion magazines at eleven. Declaring I'd own one at eighteen. Dog-earring HERLIFE for six months. Learning the business for four years. The split-second decision was the culmination of decades of preparation.

When preparation meets opportunity, that's when split-second decisions happen.

So what are you preparing for right now without knowing it? Pay attention. Study it. Practice it. Invest in it. Because one day, opportunity will show up. And you'll have about two seconds to decide if you're ready.

[YOUR TURN]

First: What's your "sell it to me" moment? What opportunity are you waiting for? What would you fight for if it became available? Be specific.

____

____

____

____

____

____

Second: Are you willing to outwork everyone else who wants what you want? What would "relentless, in the best way" look like for you?

____

____

____

____

____

____

Third: What would you leverage everything for? What's the thing you know, bone-deep, soul-certain, is yours to do?

____

____

11

AirBNB Wave

That same year I signed the papers to buy HERLIFE Magazine, I also signed papers for something else. The photography studio on Pine Street in downtown Lodi, the little house I'd been renting since 2013, the place where I'd built my photography business, I bought it. Outright. Mine. And the moment it was mine, I used it as the magazine office. This is how you use one asset to build the next. This is how you catch waves.

The studio had served its purpose. It had proven I could build a business. It had generated the income and credibility I needed to position myself to buy the magazine. But now the magazine was my focus. So the studio became the headquarters. I moved my desk into the front room where I used to do sales consultations. The back room, where I'd shot hundreds of portraits and newborns and families, became storage for back issues and supplies. The transformation happened in a weekend. And I loved every second of it.

Here's what I was learning: Nothing has to stay what it was. You can repurpose. You can pivot. You can take something that worked beautifully for one season and transform it into exactly what you need for the next.

But I wasn't done buying property. In 2018, I bought the house right next door on Pine Street. And this one? This one was a disaster too. It had been a pet grooming facility. But not a nice one. Not a place where people brought their poodles for a trim and a bow. This was a place where they (allegedly) been selling dope out of the back door, and sometimes the front door too, for twenty-five years. Where deals went down. Where people came and went at all hours. Where the neighborhood had learned to look the other way. And trying to get rid of those types of demons is a story in and of itself. There's a lot of story around business in that situation that I can teach another time.)

When I walked through it for the first time, I nearly walked back out. The floors had three layers. Somebody had laid new flooring over old flooring over the original floor, like archaeological strata of bad decisions. Twenty-five years of wet carpet compressed into a toxic lasagna of mold and stains and who-knows-what from the dog grooming. The walls were stained with nicotine and neglect. The bathroom was a horror show. The kitchen hadn't been updated since the 1970s. It smelled like failure and broken dreams.

The Voice had a lot to say about this property. This is disgusting. Why would you buy this? You're going to pour money into this pit and get nothing back. Walk away. This is too much work. But I saw something else. I saw bones.

Good bones. I saw location, prime downtown, walkable to restaurants and shops and everything tourists would want. I saw potential. And I saw a wave forming that most people weren't paying attention to yet.

Airbnb was just starting to hit the Central Valley. It was already huge in major cities, San Francisco, New York, L.A. But in smaller markets like Lodi? Most people hadn't caught on yet. This was the front of the wave in the Central Valley for Airbnb. I saw the wave. I saw the opportunity. I knew there weren't a lot of people doing it yet. There were no permits required. I recognized the wave. I jumped on it… Again.

I'd been watching the trend for a while. Reading articles. Talking to other property investors. Running the numbers. And I kept coming back to the same conclusion: This was a wave. And if I paddled out now, before everyone else figured it out, I could ride it.

The math was simple. A long-term rental in downtown Lodi might bring in $1,200 to $1,500 a month. Decent. Steady. Predictable. But an Airbnb, if you did it right, if you created an experience people actually wanted, could bring in $8,000 to $10,000 a month. For the same property. The difference wasn't the house. The difference was how you positioned it.

So I bought the disgusting pet grooming facility. And we gutted it.

Renovation is not for the faint of heart. We pulled up all three layers. Tore out the stained carpet. Ripped out the nicotine-soaked drywall. Gutted the bathroom and kitchen. What was left was bare bones. Studs and subfloor and potential.

And then we built it back up. New floors. New walls. New fixtures. We re-designed every detail, the paint colors, the furniture, the art on the walls. I wanted it to feel modern and clean and completely opposite of what it had been. I staged it like a boutique hotel room. Plush bedding. Quality towels. A fully stocked kitchen with nice dishes and real coffee. Little touches that made people feel taken care of, local guidebooks, restaurant recommendations, a basket of snacks. I didn't just want to rent a space. I wanted to create an experience. Because that's what people pay for. Not the thing itself, the feeling the thing gives them.

We got that one all dialed in. It took off. There wasn't a lot like it at that point in time. The first month it was live on Airbnb, it booked solid. Thirty consecutive days, guests typically stayed for several nights at a time, and the calendar filled up completely. Reviews started pouring in. "Beautifully designed!" "Spotless and comfortable!" "Better than a hotel!" "We'll definitely be back!" And the revenue? Exactly what I'd projected. $8,000 the first month. $9,500 the second. $10,000 the third. That property that everyone had avoided was now generating more income per month than I used to make in an entire year when I first started photography.

The Voice had nothing to say about that.

The first one was doing so well, I found another house downtown. In 2019, I bought a third property on Locust

Street. This one had an office space in the back of the house so I could work in that portion and rent the actual house out. It didn't need as much work. It was in good shape, just needed cosmetic updates, some fresh paint, better furniture. I applied the same formula: Clean, modern design. Quality everything. Attention to detail. Create an experience, not just a rental.

So I rented out the second Pine Street house as an Airbnb. That one took off too. I moved into the Locust Street office space, rented the front of the Locust Street house out as Airbnb space. All were doing eight to ten thousand a month. Within weeks, it was booked.

Now I had three Airbnb properties, all in downtown Lodi, all generating between $8,000 and $10,000 per month. That's $24,000 to $30,000 per month in rental income. While I was running a magazine.

I had three properties rolling. The magazine was doing $450,000 to $500,000 a year. The Airbnbs were generating consistent income. The farm was doing well. And I did it by leveraging one asset to the next asset to the next asset with very little money. Lots of sweat equity. A tremendous amount of determination and the fight inside of me that said I'm getting up off this mat and I am not going to lay down again.

I was the owner, editor-in-chief, and publisher of HER-LIFE Magazine, managing a team, working with over 100 advertisers, developing most of their marketing campaigns, creating content every month, running a full-scale publishing operation. And simultaneously, I was managing three short-term rental properties.

How? Because I understood something fundamental: You don't have to choose one thing. You can build multiple income streams. You can catch multiple waves. You can run several businesses at once if you're willing to work hard and build systems that don't require you to be present 24/7.

Here's how I managed it: Systems.

For the Airbnbs, I hired cleaners. Professional, reliable people who turned over each property between guests. I didn't scrub toilets myself. Well, I did at first, but the workload was too much after a while. So, I paid people who were excellent at it. I hired a handyman on retainer. If something broke, and things always break, he handled it. I got a text, I approved the repair, he took care of it. I automated everything I could. Online booking. Automatic messages to guests with check-in instructions. Smart locks so I didn't have to physically hand over keys. I designed the properties to be low-maintenance. Durable furniture. Stain-resistant fabrics. Finishes that could handle wear and tear. And I set boundaries. I checked messages twice a day, morning and evening. Unless there was an emergency, guests could wait a few hours for a response.

For the magazine, I built a similar structure. I had an editor who refined my writing. A graphic designer who handled layouts. Salespeople who pitched advertisers. A team that knew their jobs and did them well. I didn't micromanage. I hired good people, gave them clear expectations, and let them work. My job was to set the vision, make the big decisions, and keep everything moving forward. Not to do every single task myself.

This is what most people get wrong about building a business. They think they have to do it all. Be the CEO and the janitor and everything in between. But that's not sustainable. That's a recipe for burnout. The goal isn't to work harder. The goal is to build systems that work without you.

Running the Airbnbs taught me something crucial that I still use today: Opportunity hides in chaos. That pet grooming facility? Everyone else saw a mess. A problem. A property to avoid. I saw potential. The location was perfect. The bones were solid. The price was right because nobody else wanted to deal with it. So while other investors were competing for turnkey properties, bidding against each other, driving up prices, settling for slim margins, I was buying the ugly stuff nobody wanted. And I was turning it into something valuable.

This is the principle: Catch the Wave. But here's what most people miss: The biggest waves aren't the obvious ones everyone's already riding. The biggest opportunities are the ones forming just offshore. The trends most people haven't noticed yet. The ugly properties everyone's walking past. You have to train your eye to see them.

Airbnb in the Central Valley in 2018 was one of those waves. By 2021, everyone had figured it out. The marketplace was filling. Prices went down because of the increase in supply. Competition intensified. Margins got slimmer. But I'd already caught it. I'd already built my portfolio. I'd already proven the model worked. And by the time everyone else was paddling out, I was riding the wave all the way to shore.

This is strategy offered in my courses too. Not just "work hard" or "follow your passion" or any of the generic advice everyone repeats. I teach: Watch for the waves. Learn to see what others are missing. Move before the crowd figures it out. Because if you wait until everyone agrees it's a good idea, you've already missed the opportunity. The money is made on the front end of the wave, when it's still risky, when people are skeptical, when you have to have the courage to paddle out alone.

But here's the other side of catching waves that nobody talks about: You need bridges.

When I bought HERLIFE, I was taking on massive financial risk. I'd leveraged everything. If the magazine failed, I was in trouble. But the Airbnbs? Those were my bridge. They generated steady, reliable income that didn't depend on the magazine succeeding. They gave me breathing room. They created a safety net that allowed me to take bigger risks with the publishing business.

When you're transitioning from one thing to the next, from employee to entrepreneur, from one business to another, from stability to risk, you need to bridge the gap. Most people approach transitions with fear. Scarcity. "What if I can't make it work? What if I fail?" That energy is toxic. It attracts exactly what you're afraid of.

Instead, you need to fill the change with abundance. With multiple income streams. With systems that keep money flowing while you're building the next thing. The Airbnbs weren't just properties. They were my bridge. My abundance. My proof that even if one thing didn't work out, I'd be okay.

And that confidence, that lack of desperation, made everything else easier. When I was negotiating with advertisers for the magazine, I wasn't desperate for their money. I had income from other sources. So I could hold my ground, maintain my standards, walk away from deals that didn't serve me. When I was making decisions about the magazine's direction, I wasn't thinking "I have to make this work or I'll lose everything." I was thinking "I get to build this. And if it doesn't work, I have other things that are already working." That's a completely different energy. And it changes everything.

The magazine office operated from the back of that Locust Street property from 2019 until I sold HERLIFE in early 2022. Everything I touched, I tried to make it work twice as hard. The studio became the magazine office. The Airbnb property became my workspace. Every asset served multiple purposes. Every decision created multiple streams of value. This wasn't luck. This wasn't magic. This was strategy. This was seeing the waves and catching them before anyone else noticed they were forming.

My father had doubts about each property purchase. The familiar warnings about risk and failure. But I'd learned I couldn't wait for anyone's approval. The people who are actually building things don't wait for permission. They see the opportunity, run the numbers, and jump in.

Here's what I want you to understand: The people who tell you it's too risky are usually the people who've never risked anything. They're speaking from fear, not experience. They're projecting their own limitations onto you. And if you listen to them, you'll stay exactly where they are, safe, comfortable, and small.

But if you learn to see the waves, to trust your own judgment, to build bridges instead of waiting for guarantees, you can create something extraordinary. You can turn a property everyone else avoided into a revenue-generating asset. You can run multiple businesses at once. You can build wealth that doesn't depend on any single stream of income. You can write your own damn story. And if I can do it, you can too.

By the end of 2019, I was running a successful magazine, managing three Airbnb properties, raising my son Rowdy, learning about franchising and passive income models, and building confidence in myself as a businesswoman, not just a photographer. And I was just getting started.

* * *

[THE LESSON]: Catch the Wave and Build Your Bridge

See the waves before everyone else does. Watch what's working in major markets that hasn't hit smaller markets yet. Move on incomplete information instead of waiting for certainty. The biggest opportunities always come with risk, that's why most people miss them.

Opportunity hides in chaos. People who build wealth do the ugly work nobody else wants. The bigger the problem, the bigger the payoff.

Build bridges, not leaps. Keep income streams generating while building the next thing. Fill transitions with abundance, multiple income streams create confidence that changes how you negotiate and make decisions.

Use one asset to build the next. Make every asset serve multiple purposes.

[YOUR TURN]

First: What wave is forming in your industry or market that most people haven't noticed yet?

____

____

____

Second: What chaotic opportunity are you avoiding because it looks too messy?

Third: What bridge do you need to build before you make your next leap?

155

12

Having Something to Say

The first month I owned HERLIFE Magazine, I barely slept. Not because I was working around the clock, though I was. But because I was terrified. Terrified I'd made a mistake. Terrified I wasn't qualified. Terrified that everyone would see through me and realize I had no idea what I was doing. I'd leveraged everything to buy this magazine. I'd bet everything on myself. And now I had to prove I was right.

Here's what nobody tells you about buying a business: The transition is brutal. You go from watching someone else run the show to suddenly being responsible for every single decision. And the decisions never stop. Which stories should we feature this month? Which advertiser gets the back cover? Should we raise rates or keep them steady to retain clients? Do we approve this proof or send it back for revisions? How do we handle the distributor who's late with deliveries? Which photographer should shoot this cover? Do we hire this writer or find someone else? Every day brought a hundred small decisions that felt enormous. Because I was the publisher now.

The editor-in-chief. The owner. The person whose name was on the masthead. And if it failed, everyone would know.

The day I officially took over, the day Kimberly handed me the final files, the passwords, the vendor contacts, the keys to everything, I sat in the office alone after she left. Just sat there. Staring at the computer. At the filing cabinets full of contracts and invoices and years of institutional knowledge. This was mine now. All of it. Every advertiser relationship. Every reader expectation. Every deadline. Every dollar of revenue and expense. I wasn't the photographer anymore. I wasn't the consultant. I wasn't the person who got to observe from the sidelines and offer creative input. I was the boss. And the weight of that responsibility settled on my shoulders like a physical thing.

The existing team had mixed reactions. Some of them were excited. They'd worked with me for years, knew my vision, trusted that I'd bring fresh energy to the magazine. Others were cautious. Change is hard. Even when it's good change. They'd worked under Kimberly's leadership for years. They knew her systems, her preferences, her communication style. And now they had to adjust to mine. I did things differently. Made different decisions. Had different priorities. And for some people, that was uncomfortable.

A few employees didn't make the transition. They left, some because they couldn't adjust, some because they saw an opportunity elsewhere, some because the change just didn't sit right with them. I didn't take it personally. Or at least, I tried not to. But the ones who stayed? They became my allies. My core team. The people who believed in what we were building together. And slowly, we found our rhythm.

The first issue I published as owner came out in August. I must have checked the proof a hundred times before approving it for print. Scrutinizing every page. Every image. Every word. Looking for mistakes. For anything that would prove The Voice right, that I wasn't good enough, wasn't qualified, wasn't ready for this. But when the shipment arrived, when I tore open that box and pulled out the first copy with my name listed as Publisher, I cried. Happy crying. Overwhelmed crying. I-can't-believe-this-is-real crying. Because this wasn't just a magazine. This was proof. Proof that I belonged here.

But there was so much I still had to learn. When Kimberly owned the magazine, I'd watched her run it. I'd seen the moving parts. I'd asked questions. But watching someone do something and actually doing it yourself are completely different things. I had to learn fast.

Editorial: How to structure an editorial calendar months in advance. How to assign stories to writers and photographers. How to edit submissions, cutting what didn't work, strengthening what did, maintaining a consistent voice across different contributors. How to write publisher's notes that readers actually wanted to read. This last one was the hardest. Because I still carried the shame of failing English. I still heard The Voice every time I sat down to write: You can't do this. Your writing isn't good enough. People are going to see right through you.

But I had Marilyn.

Marilyn was my copy editor. Older. Seasoned. Wise. The kind of editor who'd seen everything and knew exactly how to fix it. And I was constantly apologizing to her. Every time I handed her my publisher's note, I'd preface it with disclaimers. "I know this isn't good." "I'm so sorry, I know it's a mess. I know I don't understand writing." "Thank you for putting up with me. Do your best with it." I felt like a burden. Like I was asking her to turn garbage into gold every single month.

But Marilyn never made me feel small. She'd read my drafts, these raw, heartfelt, messy attempts at connecting with readers, and she'd say, "This is good. Your voice is strong. You're saying something real here." And then she'd work her magic. Tightening sentences. Fixing grammar. Smoothing out the rough edges. But the heart of what I'd written? She kept that intact.

One month, after I'd handed her a particularly vulnerable piece, something about overcoming shame and finding your voice, she looked at me and said: "Dee, having something to say is more important than perfect grammar."

I stared at her.

"Your readers don't care if every comma is in the right place," she continued. "They care that you're being real with them. That you're sharing something that matters. That's what connects. Not perfection. Truth."

That landed in my chest and stayed there. For years, I'd been fighting the shame of failing English. Fighting the belief that I wasn't smart enough, wasn't educated enough, wasn't qualified to write anything people would want to read. But Marilyn showed me something different.

So I put all my ideas and all my thoughts onto paper with great vulnerability, great emotion, great purity, great authenticity. And she fixed the technical writing aspect of it. Then it would come back to me and I would read it and I would learn how to fix it. I would learn how she cleaned that up. I would learn how she saw it in the technical aspect and I became a better writer because of that. I started learning technicality because she would edit my work.

And my writing was well received because it came from authenticity. It came from purity of heart. The highest frequency you can have. I wrote from love. And it didn't matter if I was technically sound because I certainly wasn't. I learned to not worry about it because I hired the right people to clean that up. And that's what happened.

And I became more confident because of it. And I wrote more. And I wrote more. And I wrote more. And then I developed confidence and I said, I can do this. This is a skill I can do. I am a writer. I'm published every single month. I'm a published writer.

Graphic Design: I had to learn how layouts worked. Not just "this looks nice," but why certain compositions drew the eye, how to balance text and images, how to create flow so readers naturally moved from one story to the next. I studied typography. Color theory. The subtle art of making pages look professional without looking cluttered. Every month, I'd work with our graphic designer, learning her language, understanding how she thought about space and hierarchy and visual storytelling. I'd bring her my vision for a cover or a spread, and she'd translate it into something polished and magazine-worthy. And slowly, I started to see pages the way she saw them. To understand that design isn't just decoration, it's communication.

Sales: This was where my photography studio experience paid off. I already knew how to sell. How to build relationships. How to present value. How to close. But selling advertising space in a magazine was different from selling portrait sessions. I had to learn media kits. Rate cards. Circulation numbers. Demographic breakdowns. How to price based on placement and size and frequency. I had to learn how to negotiate with advertisers who wanted discounts, who wanted to trade services instead of paying cash, who wanted custom packages that didn't exist in our standard offerings. I had to learn how to say no. How to hold firm on pricing. How to walk away from deals that weren't worth it. And I had to learn how to say yes, how to recognize good clients, how to build long-term partnerships, how to create win-win relationships that benefited both the magazine and the advertiser.

By the end of the first year, I had over 100 advertising clients. Some small local businesses buying quarter-page ads. Some major regional brands taking full pages or spreads. Some national accounts that came through the franchise network.

Each one represented a relationship I'd built. A pitch I'd made. A value proposition I'd sold. And each one was proof that I could do this.

Operations: This was the unglamorous side of publishing. Printer relationships. Distribution logistics. Shipping schedules. Inventory management. Making sure the magazine got from the printer to the distributors to the waiting rooms and mailboxes and newsstands where readers would find it. And let me tell you: shipping was a constant nightmare. We were always coming up against deadlines. Always dealing with trucking companies that were late or lost shipments or delivered to the wrong locations. I swear I got so much gray hair just from managing shipping and delivery. There were months when I'd be on the phone with the printer at 10 PM, trying to figure out if we could make the deadline. Calling the distributor at 6 AM to confirm the truck was actually on its way. It was stressful. Relentless. Exhausting. But it was also critical. Because none of the beautiful design or compelling content or hard-won advertising mattered if the magazine didn't actually reach readers. So I learned operations. I built systems. I found vendors I could trust and held them accountable when they dropped the ball.

Finances: I learned how to read a P&L. How to manage cash flow. How to forecast revenue and expenses months in advance. How to make hard decisions when the numbers didn't work out the way I'd hoped. Do we cut this expense? Raise rates? Find new revenue streams? Tighten the budget somewhere else? Every month, I'd sit down with the financials and ask myself: Is this sustainable? Are we growing? Are we profitable? And I'd make adjustments. Because the creative side of publishing is fun. It's exciting. It's what drew me to magazines in the first place. But the business side is what keeps the lights on. And I had to master both. That first year, the magazine brought in strong revenue, approaching seven figures annually. The magazine was already healthy when I bought it, Kimberly had built something strong and sustainable. But I didn't just maintain what she'd created. I grew it. I brought my vision. My energy. My willingness to push boundaries and take risks. And it worked.

But success doesn't come without stumbling blocks. And my first big crisis taught me exactly what kind of publisher I was going to be.

I'd commissioned a fashion editorial for one of the early issues under my ownership. Beautiful photography. Gorgeous jewelry. High-end styling. And one of the shots featured a model in a bra, tasteful, artistic, but yes, showing cleavage, wearing this stunning statement necklace. I loved it. It was exactly the kind of edgier, bolder aesthetic I wanted to bring to the magazine. So we published it.

And then the calls started.

One of our largest advertisers, a medical institution with hospitals, doctors' offices, and clinics, placed significant advertising with us every month. Thousands of dollars in revenue. And they distributed our magazines in all their waiting rooms. Apparently, when that issue came out, it went to their board. And the board had a meltdown. They were outraged. Offended. Scandalized by the image of a woman in her bra. And they didn't just pull our magazines from the waiting rooms. They went through every single magazine in every office and physically tore out the pages with that fashion editorial.

Then they called me. "We can't have this kind of content in our facilities," they said. "Our patients are conservative. This is inappropriate. We're reconsidering our advertising contract."

And it wasn't just the medical institution. We had older subscribers, women who'd been reading the magazine for years, call to cancel their subscriptions. "This is too risqué." "I didn't sign up for this." "What happened to the magazine I loved?"

The Voice had a field day. See? You pushed too hard. You went too far. You ruined it. Kimberly never would have done this. You're going to lose everything because you couldn't just play it safe.

But here's what's interesting: For every person who complained, I gained ten new subscribers. The whole point of that editorial, the whole point of pushing boundaries, was to attract a new audience. A younger demographic. Readers who wanted something bolder, fresher, more visually interesting than the safe, conservative content they could find anywhere else. And it worked. Our subscriber base grew substantially after that issue. New advertisers reached out, brands that wanted to be associated with the edgier direction we were taking. Younger readers started following us on social media, engaging with our content, sharing our posts.

For every critic, there were far more supporters. The people who love what you're doing don't always call to tell you. They just quietly subscribe. Buy. Engage. Stay. It's the critics who make noise. But the supporters? They vote with their wallets. And the numbers proved I'd made the right call.

The medical institution stayed on as an advertiser, by the way. After the initial outrage settled, they realized we were reaching their target demographic in ways their own marketing couldn't. They adjusted. Set clearer boundaries about what could appear in the copies distributed in their facilities. And we kept doing business together. Because at the end of the day, results matter more than comfort.

Stumbling wasn't always external. Sometimes it came from the people closest to me. I had an assistant who'd been with me for a while. Someone I trusted. Someone I considered a friend. And she was stealing from me. Not all at once. Not in obvious ways. She was "fat-fingering" the ledgers, adjusting numbers here and there, skimming a little off the top, making it look like accounting errors or discrepancies. Over the course of a year, she took a substantial amount of money. I didn't catch it immediately. Because I trusted her. Because I was busy running the magazine and managing the Airbnbs and raising Rowdy. But eventually, the numbers didn't add up. And when I started digging, I found it.

That was one of the hardest lessons I've ever had to learn. Not just about business, about people. About the fact that you can care about someone, trust them, treat them well, and they can still betray you. I fired her. Obviously. And I put systems in place to make sure it couldn't happen again. But it hurt. Not just financially. Personally. Because I'd let her in. I'd valued her. I'd trusted her. And she'd taken advantage of that.

And it wasn't just her. I had delivery people who threw magazines away instead of distributing them. People who stole magazines to sell or keep for themselves. People who collected payment for work they never actually did. Every time it happened, I learned. I learned to call out problems faster. To trust my instincts when something felt off. To put systems in place that made theft harder and accountability clearer. I learned that kindness doesn't mean being a pushover. That you can care about people and still hold them to high standards. That protecting your business isn't mean, it's necessary.

People ask me all the time: "How do you do it all?" And the answer is: Systems. I didn't do everything myself. I couldn't. I hired cleaners for the Airbnbs. I hired a copy editor for the magazine. I delegated operations tasks. I automated what could be automated. I built systems that didn't require me to be present 24/7. Because the truth is, you can run multiple businesses, but only if you're not the bottleneck. Only if you build infrastructure that works whether you're there or not.

And through it all, I kept learning about franchising. HERLIFE was part of a franchise network. And as the owner of a franchised location, I got to see how the whole system worked. How franchisors established new franchisees. How they licensed ideas and intellectual property. How they collected royalties, typically 10-15% of gross revenue. How, if you built the right model, you could create passive income at scale. The franchisor wasn't doing the day-to-day work in each market. They were providing the brand, the systems, the support. And they were collecting a percentage from every franchisee. Which meant that if you had ten franchisees each doing substantial revenue, you were collecting significant passive income per market. Scale that to twenty markets? Thirty? Fifty? You're looking at multi-million-dollar annual income without having to run the day-to-day operations. I filed that knowledge away. I wasn't ready to build a franchise myself yet. But I understood the model. I saw how powerful it could be. And I knew, someday, I'd use what I was learning.

Every month when a new issue came out, I tore open that box with the same excitement as the first time. It never got old. Holding that magazine in my hands. Seeing the cover I'd art-directed. The stories I'd assigned. The publisher's note I'd written. Seeing my vision come to life on glossy pages. And I'd sit with Kimberly, yes, even after I became the owner, and we'd go through each issue together. What worked. What didn't. What we could improve. What we should do more of. She remained my confidant. My sounding board. My friend. And we still do this today with Ropers Sports News Magazine. Every issue, we review it together. Because having someone who understands the work, who cares about the craft, who'll tell you the truth, that's invaluable.

I also learned something critical during those years: Living in someone else's shadow isn't failure. It's just part of the journey. There were advertisers who could never be as happy with me as they were with Kimberly. They'd worked with her for years. They trusted her. They knew her style. And I was different. I made different decisions. I had different priorities. I brought different energy. And for some people, that just didn't work.

But here's what I discovered: For every advertiser who preferred Kimberly, there was an advertiser who only wanted to work with me. People who were drawn to my vision. My boldness. My willingness to take risks and push boundaries. It's the law of attraction. You attract your people. And you repel the people who aren't meant for you. And that's okay. You're not trying to be everything to everyone. You're trying to be the right thing for the right people.

By the end of that first year, I'd proven something to myself: I could do this. I could run a magazine. I could lead a team. I could manage finances and operations and sales and editorial. I could handle crisis. I could make hard decisions. I could learn on the fly and adapt when things didn't go as planned. I wasn't just maintaining what Kimberly had built. I was building my own version of it. My voice. My vision. My magazine.

And The Voice, the one that had screamed at me for years that I wasn't qualified, wasn't educated enough, wasn't good enough, was finally starting to quiet down. Not because I'd become perfect. But because I'd become proof. Proof that mastery matters more than credentials. Proof that having something to say is more important than saying it perfectly. Proof that you don't need permission to build something extraordinary. You just need to show up. Do the work. Learn as you go. And refuse to quit when it gets hard.

* * *

[THE LESSON]: Mastery Gives Value That Education Cannot

Mastery comes from doing, not from degrees. Learn by making decisions, dealing with consequences, and figuring it out in real time. Put in your 10,000 hours actually doing the work, making mistakes, and solving problems nobody taught you how to solve.

Having something to say matters more than saying it perfectly. Raw, honest, vulnerable content resonates more than technically perfect but soulless writing. Your voice is more valuable than perfect grammar.

You don't have to choose one thing. Build systems that don't require you to be present 24/7. Hire people for specific tasks. Delegate operations. Automate processes. You can run multiple businesses if you're not the bottleneck.

Crisis reveals what you're made of. Every crisis is an opportunity to prove you can handle it. Crisis doesn't destroy you, it refines you.

And always double-check the numbers. You are the only one that controls what goes out. You are the only one that signs the checks. Full stop.

[YOUR TURN]

First: What are you learning by doing right now? What skill are you building through action rather than study?

____

____

____

____

____

Second: What do you have to say that only you can say? What truth or experience or perspective is uniquely yours?

____

____

____

____

____

Third: What systems could you build to multiply your impact without multiplying your time?

____

____

____

Bent Knee

For years, I ran HERLIFE Magazine like a machine. Every month, a new issue. Every month, new advertisers. Every month, the magazine landing in thousands of homes and businesses across the Central Valley. The revenue was strong. The team was solid. The systems worked. From the outside, it looked like I'd made it. I was running the Airbnb properties. I had a substantial book of clients who trusted me, paid me, came back month after month. But something was shifting. Slowly at first. Then faster. And by 2020, I could feel it. Everyone could feel it.

Rowdy was struggling in school. Had been for years, actually. My son has a complex form of dyslexia, severe enough that he needs to see a word 350 times before he can remember it. Names, words, basic associations that most kids take for granted? For Rowdy, they're a daily battle. Add ADHD to that mix, and you have a kid who doesn't fit the traditional classroom mold. He flipped words. He couldn't keep up with reading assignments. He struggled to communicate verbally the way teachers expected.

And the system, both public and private, wanted to fix him with pharmaceuticals. "Put him on medication," they said. "It'll help him focus. It'll make him easier to manage." But I refused. I'd watched too many kids get medicated into compliance and struggle with addiction later in life. Watched their spark dim. Watched them become versions of themselves that fit the system but lost something essential in the process. I wasn't going to do that to my son.

So I fought.

We started in public school when Rowdy was young. And that system, it wanted to inhale my son, digest him, and spit him out because he didn't fit their mold. They didn't know what to do with a bright, creative kid whose brain worked differently. So they labeled him. Tested him. Tried to push medication. I pulled him out.

We went to private Christian school. Smaller classes. More individual attention. Surely they could handle a student who thought differently. But they couldn't. Or wouldn't. That system didn't want the challenge of a student who didn't fit their template either. Maybe it would be different. It wasn't. The stress was tremendous. The failures kept piling up. The constant meetings with teachers, administrators, specialists, all telling me the same thing: Your son needs medication. Your son needs to conform. Your son needs to fit our system.

But what about a system that fits my son?

When you have a child with learning disabilities, the pressure to medicate is relentless. From the time children are born they are trying to poke, prod, and dose them to death. Literally. Because a medicated child is easier to manage. Quieter. More compliant. Less disruptive to the classroom flow. And more dependent on the system.

I kept thinking about how my creative brain didn't work the way teachers expected. About how I was made to feel stupid, inadequate, broken. And I realized: Rowdy's brain works like mine. He's creative. "He's smart, so smart that his brain moves faster than his mouth can keep up, which is why he flips words." He doesn't have a deficit. He has a different operating system. And the school system, built for one type of learner, built to produce employees, couldn't handle it. Couldn't handle him. Couldn't handle independent, self-reliant thinking.

So I made a decision. Fall 2020, in the midst of all the chaos: I brought Rowdy home. Homeschooled him. Best decision I ever made.

People ask me all the time: "How did you do it? How do you do all you do, and homeschool your son?" The honest answer is: I bought his education. I hired tutors. I found curriculum that worked for his brain. I built a learning environment that didn't require him to conform to someone else's template. I taught him how to think. How to problem-solve. How to ask the right questions. We started three businesses together during those homeschool years. I taught him website building. Marketing. How to take an idea from concept to execution. And I watched him flourish. Not because I'm a certified teacher. But because

I refused to let the system tell me what my son needed, I and that he couldn't do some thing.

[internal dialogue: Hold my beer while I teach him how to be a superstar!]

I became an advocate, not just for Rowdy, but for other mothers making similar decisions. Fighting similar battles. Refusing to medicate their kids into compliance. This is a story that deserves its own book too. The full complexity of navigating the school system, fighting for your child, choosing education over medication, that's bigger than what we can cover here. But know this: it shaped everything that came next.

Because bringing Rowdy home forced me to look in the mirror. And ask: Who have I become?

I was running myself into the ground. The magazine. The Airbnbs. Homeschool. The ranch. Clients demanding my attention. I was successful by every external measure. But internally? I was exhausted. And worse, I was starting to lose my voice.

It was 2020. The world was changing. Fast. Lockdowns. Mandates. The entire social and political landscape shifting in ways nobody had predicted. And I had opinions about it. Strong opinions. About freedom. About government overreach. About natural immunity and bodily autonomy and the right to make your own health decisions. About natural health. About spirituality. I wrote about it in my publisher's notes. Bold. Unapologetic. Real.

And my readers loved it. They wrote me emails saying "Thank you for saying what we're all thinking." They told me the magazine felt like a breath of fresh air in a world gone mad.

But my advertisers? Some of them didn't love it.

And it landed like a bomb.

One of my biggest advertisers was a hospital system. A conglomerate with substantial marketing dollars. All of the Central Valley hospital systems had full-page ads with me. The magazine was making money. And then the vice president, a friend I'd known for a long time, called me. Furious. She was pulling all of her advertising because of my messaging.

I begged her to meet with me so we could talk. I was trying to save this relationship. I was also looking to keep that magazine afloat because I could see what was happening in our society and the economic picture and I was concerned. I was concerned about what was going to happen to that business because the first thing to go in any company is the marketing budget.

The coffee shop was one of those trendy local places with outdoor seating under a sprawling oak tree, the kind of spot where people usually lingered over lattes and talked about nothing important. It was a beautiful day. Warm sun filtering through the leaves, a gentle breeze moving through the patio, everything around us alive and normal and completely at odds with what was about to happen.

She showed up in a mask. I was not in a mask. I refused to wear a mask. Judge me, hate me, love me, whatever, that's just how I felt. The contrast was immediate, visual, a line drawn between us before either of us said a word. I stood to greet her, awkward, unsure if I should hug her or keep my distance. She stayed back. The tension was thick. I could feel it in my chest, in the way my hands fumbled as I offered to buy her coffee. She nodded, didn't smile. I went inside, ordered, paid, came back out to the table where she was already sitting, stiff, waiting.

We sat outside in that beautiful sunshine, and she kept her mask on the entire time. I could see her eyes, hard and unyielding, but I couldn't read her expression fully. Couldn't see if her mouth was tight with anger or if she was struggling with this too. The mask created a barrier, not just physical but emotional. I was speaking freely, my face exposed, vulnerable, trying to connect, trying to explain, trying to save what we'd built together over the years. And she sat there, covered, protected, unmoved.

I started with an apology. For something I wasn't sorry for. "I didn't mean to offend you," I said, hearing how hollow it sounded even as the words left my mouth. "I value our partnership. I've always valued it."

She didn't soften. "Your publisher's notes have been problematic."

"I hear you," I said, leaning forward, trying to bridge the distance between us. "And I want to understand. Help me understand your marketing campaign. I don't think I fully grasped what you were trying to communicate."

"We're in the business of selling COVID right now," she said. Plain. Direct. No softening. "That's what we're doing. Our entire marketing campaign is based on interventions for COVID. Testing. Treatment. Vaccines. We need to make sure we're selling COVID. And we can't have you speaking against it."

I felt the ground shift under me. "I'm not speaking against healthcare," I said carefully. "I'm speaking about freedom. About personal choice. About bodily autonomy."

"Which contradicts our messaging."

"But we've worked together for years," I said, and I could hear the desperation creeping into my voice. "You know me. You know my heart. You know I'm not trying to hurt your business. This magazine has always been a platform for different voices, different perspectives. That's what makes it valuable."

"And your voice is your discretion," she said evenly.

"Exactly," I said, grasping at that. "My voice is my discretion. I'm the publisher. I have editorial freedom to say what I believe."

She paused. Let that hang in the air between us. And then she said it. "Yes. Your voice is to your discretion. However, I don't have to advertise with you. And I'm not going to if that's going to be your discretion."

The words hit like a slap. Clean. Clear. Final.

"Please," I said, and I hated the sound of my own voice. "Don't pull out. You've been with me since the beginning. You know what this magazine means to the community. You know the reach we have."

"I do know," she said. "Which is why your messaging is so concerning."

"What if I'm more careful?" I offered, scrambling. "What if I choose my words differently? I'm not trying to undermine what you're doing. I just want to give voice to people who feel like they're not being heard."

"The people you're giving voice to are speaking against public health measures."

"They're speaking about their own bodies. Their own choices."

"Which impacts our ability to market our services."

I sat back, staring at her across that little table. The coffee between us going cold. The sun still warm on my shoulders. The breeze still moving through the oak leaves above us. Everything so normal. Everything so wrong.

"I need you to understand something," I said quietly. "The economy is shifting. Advertising budgets are going to tighten.

I know that. I can feel it happening already. And I know that advertising is one of the first things businesses cut when things get uncertain. Losing your account…" I stopped, swallowed hard. "It could start a domino effect. Other businesses will see you pull out and they'll question whether they should stay too."

She didn't respond. Just watched me.

"So I'm asking you," I continued. "Please. Stay with me. Give me a chance to figure this out. We can make this work."

"Can we?" she asked. "Because from where I'm sitting, you're going to keep writing what you believe, and what you believe is bad for my business."

"What if I don't?" The words came out before I could stop them. "What if I pull back on those topics? What if I focus on other things? The magazine is about women's health, women's lives, community connection. There's so much else I can write about."

She tilted her head slightly, considering. "You'd do that?"

And there it was. The moment. The choice. The line I was about to cross.

"Yes," I said. "I would do that. To keep you. To keep this partnership. I would do that."

I watched her relax slightly. Saw the tension ease in her

shoulders. Knew I'd given her what she wanted.

"Alright," she said. "Then we can continue. But I need you to understand that I'll be watching. If your messaging shifts back to what it was, we're done. No second chances."

"I understand," I said.

And I did understand. I understood exactly what I'd just done. I'd sold my voice for a contract. I'd chosen fear over faith. I'd bent a knee to keep the peace, to keep the money, to keep the lights on.

It felt as if, I bent a knee to Satan himself in that moment for money. I bent a knee to authenticity, to true alignment of myself, to true alignment of my voice for money.

And the worst part? She knew it. I could see it in her eyes, even through the mask. She didn't respect me more for bending. She respected me less. Because now she knew. My voice had a price. My values were negotiable. I could be controlled.

I drove home from that coffee shop in a fog. The sun was still shining, the day still beautiful, but I felt like I was moving through a different world than everyone else. I got in my truck and I just sat there for a moment before starting the engine, staring at the steering wheel, trying to process what I'd just done. I speak my face was hot, my pulse was racing, and I had to face myself. I was mad. At her. At the situation. At myself. Mostly at myself

The drive back to the ranch was a blur. I don't remember the roads. I don't remember the turns. I just remember gripping the steering wheel and feeling this suffocating weight settling over my chest. By the time I pulled into the driveway, I was numb. I walked into the house, and Ronnie looked at me, started to ask how it went, and I couldn't even speak. I just shook my head and walked past him. I went into my office, closed the door, and sat in my chair in the dark.

And I cried. Not the loud, cathartic kind of crying that releases something. The quiet, hollow kind. The kind that comes when you've betrayed yourself and you know it. When you've compromised on something that matters and there's no taking it back. I had spent years building a voice that mattered. Years earning the trust of readers who counted on me to say what they were thinking. Years creating a space where truth still meant something. And in one conversation, over coffee, under a beautiful oak tree on a perfect day, I'd given it all away.

The thing is, I knew better. I knew that bending the knee never stops at just once. I knew that once you establish that your integrity is for sale, people will keep coming back to negotiate the price. I knew that respect isn't earned through compliance. I knew all of this. And I did it anyway. Because I was tired. Because I was scared. Because I convinced myself it was the smart business decision. Because I told myself that keeping the lights on mattered more than keeping my voice.

But my spirit knew the truth. And it absolutely trashed me.

That did something to me that I never knew would happen. It

crushed my soul. It crushed my creativity. This is 2021. I've got a lot of businesses rolling. I've got a lot of clients. My reputation matters to me. Your reputation in your network matters when you don't come from much. Your reputation and your good word is what you have. Your network is established on your good word and your reputation.

And I never spoke truly again in that magazine.

You could see it in the light of my words. You could see it in the energy of the message. You could see that I was broke, I was broken, I was broken in spirit. She broke me. Actually, I broke myself, because you always have opportunity. You're the problem and the resolve. I can't blame her. She had a job to do. It was my decision to bend a knee for that advertising money. It is something that I've had to reckon with, had to look at, had to observe.

The joy I'd felt building that publication, the excitement of every new issue, the pride of every cover, the connection with readers who trusted my voice, it all turned painful. The thing I'd loved became the thing I dreaded.

It got worse; Because of the "Pandemic," Customers I'd known for years wouldn't see me anymore. I was someone who showed up in person, shook hands, sat across the table and listened to what people needed. That was how I did business. But suddenly, people were afraid to let me into their offices. Afraid to be near me. People I'd built relationships with over a decade.

I spiraled. I went quiet, introverted. The woman who'd always had something to say suddenly had nothing left to give. I didn't want to work in the Central Valley anymore. The town that my family was a part of for generations shut down and turned their backs on business owners. Clients were losing their minds, and I had no interest in playing in that matrix anymore.

The second I bent that knee, something inside me died.

Not dramatically. Not all at once. But slowly, over the months that followed, the light went out. Writing publisher's notes used to energize me. It was my chance to connect with readers, to be real, to say the things that mattered. But now? It felt like a performance. Like I was playing a character. Like I was editing my truth for a paycheck. And my spirit knew. Even when I tried to pretend it was fine, even when I told myself it was just business, even when I rationalized that compromise is part of running a company, my spirit knew.

I couldn't write freely. I couldn't photograph freely. Women were wearing masks on photo sessions and I had to tap dance around them. I had to tap dance around getting that work done. What the hell was I doing? I didn't believe in the campaigns these systems were selling. I didn't belong in this business anymore.

Success that costs you your voice is just a prettier cage.

I kept running the magazine through 2021. Kept publishing. Kept selling ads. Kept going through the motions. But I wasn't present anymore. Not really. I was doing the work. But the joy was gone. Marilyn could see it. She'd edit my publisher's notes and say gently, "This doesn't sound like you." Kimberly could see it. We'd review an issue together and she'd ask, "Are you okay?" The engagement dropped. Because they could feel it too. I wasn't being real anymore. And if I wasn't being real, what was the point?

By late 2021, I knew. I had to sell the magazine.

Not because it wasn't profitable. It was still making money. Not because I couldn't do the work. I could. But because I couldn't keep doing work that required me to silence myself. And I couldn't watch our community boil down to a shadow of what it once was. Weak. Compromised. Lost. I'd managed HERLIFE on authenticity. On connection. On saying things that mattered. And the moment I started editing my truth for advertising dollars, I lost the very thing that made the magazine worth building.

I called a woman who had been interested in buying the magazine years prior and asked her if she was still interested. She had publishing experience. She understood the business. And she wanted HERLIFE. She jumped at the opportunity and offered me a solid amount for the magazine. The negotiations were straightforward. She knew what she was buying. I knew what I was letting go. I had already been through the transition with Kimberly. I knew how to streamline it into a new ownership.

In early 2022, I sold HERLIFE Magazine to her. One of the

hardest decision I ever made. And the right one.

People asked me: "Why would you sell something so success-ful? Why walk away?" And I told them the truth: Because success means nothing if you lose your authentic voice along the way. I'd rather have less money and my integrity than all the money in the world and a silenced spirit. I'd rather build something new, something I could be fully honest in, than keep running something that required me to perform. I'd rather write my own story than let advertisers write it for me.

The day I signed the papers, I cried. Not sad crying. Relief crying. Because I'd been carrying weight I didn't realize was crushing me. The weight of maintaining success that didn't feel like mine anymore. The weight of showing up for a business I'd fallen out of love with. The weight of pretending everything was fine when it wasn't. And now? I was free. Free to figure out what came next. Free to rebuild on my own terms. Free to use my voice again. Free to write the next chapter of my story.

Looking back, I can see what 2020-2022 taught me: You can have all the external success in the world, the money, the business, the clients, the reputation, and still be completely empty inside. Because success without authenticity isn't success. It's just a discreet version of selling out. And I'd done enough of that.

The girl who failed English, who survived loss, who rebuilt from nothing, who fought for her son's education, that girl wasn't going to spend the rest of her life playing small to keep advertisers happy. I was ready to return to photography. To storytelling. To the cowgirl work that had always made me come alive, those images I'd captured years before, that body of work waiting to become something more. I was ready to go home and rest and reset. And I did just that.

* * *

[THE LESSON]: Wrong Path Feels Wrong, Even When It Looks Right

Your body knows before your brain does. If you're successful but exhausted, something's wrong. If you're making money but miserable, trust the feeling. External markers of success don't mean anything if you've lost yourself in the process.

Bending the knee is never worth it. When you compromise your truth for money, you lose the very thing that made you valuable. Once you've established that your integrity is negotiable, people will keep negotiating.

People respect conviction, not compliance. When you bend the knee, people don't respect you more, they respect you less. They know you can be controlled. They know your voice has a price.

Sometimes you have to burn it down to build something better. The thing you worked hardest to build can become the thing holding you back from what you're meant to do next.

[YOUR TURN]

First: What external success are you chasing that doesn't actually feel good?

Second: Where have you bent the knee? Where have you silenced yourself to keep the peace or keep the money?

Third: What do you need to burn down to build something better?

____

____

____

14

Coming Home

The world shut down. Schools closed. Businesses closed. Everyone retreated to their homes, scared and uncertain and waiting for someone to tell them what to do next. But for us? It wasn't a shutdown. It was a homecoming. Rowdy's school closed, and we brought him home. And we never went back. Not to school. Not to town. Not to the frantic pace of running between work and obligations and activities that filled our calendar but emptied our souls. We came home. To the ranch. To each other. To the land. And we stayed.

The transition was harder than I expected. Not logistically, we had space, we had animals, we had everything we needed to sustain ourselves. But neurologically? Emotionally? It was like our nervous systems didn't know how to slow down. We'd been running at full speed for so long, me with the magazine, Ronnie with his contracting work, Rowdy with school and activities, that stopping felt violent. Like slamming on the brakes at 80 miles per hour. We were restless. Irritable. Trying to fill the silence with noise because silence felt wrong.

But slowly, day by day, week by week, we recalibrated. We had to reacquaint ourselves with each other. With who we were when we weren't performing. When we weren't hustling. When we weren't trying to prove something to the world.

We shut the TV off. We stopped watching the news. Haven't watched it since. Because the noise outside our ranch, the fear, the panic, the division, it wasn't helping. It was poison. And we'd had enough poison.

By 2021, Ronnie quit the big job he was on. They wanted him to bend his knee. To comply with mandates he didn't agree with. To choose a paycheck over his principles. And he said no. Just like I'd said no when I sold HERLIFE rather than keep silencing my voice. We were done compromising. Done letting other people dictate how we lived, what we believed, what we were allowed to say.

So Ronnie came home too. And suddenly, for the first time in our marriage, we were all together. All the time. No commutes. No schedules dictated by someone else. No splitting our attention between work and home. Just us. The ranch. The land. The work.

Our ranch is in a county that stayed free during those years. While other places locked down, mandated masks, enforced restrictions, our county said: No. We trust people to make their own decisions. And that freedom? That mattered more than I can describe. Because it meant we could live the way we believed was right. We could gather. We could work. We could worship. We could raise our son without fear that someone would report us for not complying.

And in that freedom, something shifted. Everything slowed down. But we also stuck together. Deeply. Fiercely. Intentionally. We realized: We are stronger together. Our bond as a family, tested by financial stress, by years of running in different directions, that bond tightened. We became a unit again. Not just people living in the same house. But a family fighting on the same team. And it healed something in me I didn't even know was broken.

I found myself without any career, which was really strange because I had been working since I was really young. I mean, even before I was seventeen, taking my first photography job at eighteen, I worked for my grandmother in her store. I started working for her at thirteen years old until I went to work doing photography. So I had been working since I was thirteen years old, and now I found myself home with nothing but my son and my family and silence.

And so I reacquainted myself with myself. And with my family and God and the land. And I was happy. I was happy I did it.

Homesteading practices run deep in my family. My grandparents knew how to live off the land. How to grow food, preserve it, make everything from scratch. How to be self-sufficient in ways most people have forgotten. I'd been taught these things as a young girl. Watched my grandmother can vegetables. Helped in gardens. Learned the rhythms of planting and harvesting and putting food by for winter. But I'd always been too busy to really practice it. Too focused on building businesses, chasing success, proving myself.

Now? I had time. And I used it.

We filled the ranch with life. Horses. Cows. Chickens. Dogs. I reworked the orchard I'd been building since we moved there in 2015. Pruned trees. Amended soil. Planned what would fruit when so we'd have fresh food nearly year-round. I built a gigantic garden. I'd had a small garden before. But now I made it enormous. Sprawling. Abundant. I planted everything. Tomatoes, peppers, squash, beans, lettuce, herbs, root vegetables and even things I'd never grown before but wanted to learn. I saved all my seeds. Studied crop rotation. Made irrigation my life, learning which plants needed what, when, how much. And then I preserved everything I grew. Canned it. Fermented it. Dried it. Froze it.

I made homemade dinners every single night. Not from a box or a package. From our land. We processed our own meat. Had our own eggs. Raised broods of chicks and watched them grow into laying hens. I bred dogs, bird dogs for hunters who wanted quality animals.

I became a fermented foods expert. Sauerkraut, kimchi, pickles, kombucha. Learning the old ways of preserving food that also heal your gut, build your immune system, keep you strong. I became a tincture aficionado. Growing herbs, making extracts, learning which plants heal what ailments. My dad taught me how to make distilled spirits, and I used them for extraction. For pulling the medicinal properties out of plants and preserving them. I made fermented sourdough bread daily. Real bread. The kind that takes time and attention and feeds your body instead of just filling your stomach.

And my body changed. I gained 40 pounds in those years. Not from eating junk. From eating real food. From slowing down. From not being stressed to the point of physical breakdown. My body finally felt safe enough to rest. And I let it. I stopped obsessing over my appearance. Stopped buying things and clothes I used to be addicted to. Because none of that mattered anymore.

What mattered was: Could I grow food? Could I preserve it? Could I keep my family healthy and fed and strong? That was wealth. That was success. Not the number on a scale or the label on my jeans.

I started rituals that grounded me. Outdoor mineral baths daily. Soaking in hot water under the sky, letting the tension leave my body. Sungazing every morning. Standing barefoot on the earth, watching the sun rise, letting that light reset my circadian rhythm. Riding horses. Not for sport. For connection. For the feeling of working with an animal that's bigger than you, stronger than you, but chooses to partner with you. Playing with dogs. Hugging trees, yes, literally. Because there's something about wrapping your arms around something ancient and alive that reminds you you're not alone.

Praying every day. Not performative prayer. Not church-appropriate prayer. Just me and God and the land and the truth.

I stopped drinking alcohol completely. Because I didn't need it anymore. Didn't need to numb or escape or unwind with a substance. The ranch unwound me. The work unwound me. The slowness unwound me.

I made grounding and prayer a priority. Not something I did when I had time. But the thing everything else was built around. I slowed down my cussing. Not completely, I'm still me. But I became more intentional about my words. Because words matter. They shape reality. They create energy. And I wanted to create something different than what I'd been creating.

I learned every plant and animal species that lived on our ranch. Intimately. Not just their names. But their habits. Their needs. Their patterns. I learned which birds showed up when. Which plants grew where. Which insects were beneficial and which were pests. I learned to read the land the way I used to read people. To see what it was telling me. To respond to what it needed.

And in return, the land fed us. Healed us. Held us.

This is what emotional mastery looks like. Not controlling your emotions. But creating a life where you don't need to control them because you're finally living in alignment. I didn't heal from bending the knee at HERLIFE by talking about it or processing it or going to therapy. I healed by creating something new. By pouring myself into the Cowgirl

Culture book. By never looking back. By building a life that didn't require me to compromise.

The ranch gave me that. The land didn't care about my revenue numbers or my client count or whether I was successful by the world's standards. The land cared about: Did I show up? Did I do the work? Did I tend what needed tending? And when I did, it gave back.

During those years, I also became obsessed with law. Constitutional law. Trust law. Contract law. Business structure. I studied for hours. Days. Months. Because I realized: everything I'd known about business structure was no longer serving me or my family. The way I'd been operating, the entities I'd set up, the way I held assets, the way I paid taxes, it was leaving us vulnerable. And I was done being vulnerable.

So I learned how to restructure everything. On paper. Legally. Strategically. I learned how to remove myself from systems I no longer wanted to participate in. How to protect what we'd built. How to pass it on to Rowdy in a way that wouldn't be destroyed by taxes or litigation or government overreach. The depth of what I learned, the way I restructured our entire life, it's too much for one chapter. But it mattered. Because knowledge is power. And I was done being powerless.

And I watched my son become a man.

Rowdy started a beekeeping business during those years. Ronnie and I went with him everywhere, to apiaries, to workshops, to meetings with other beekeepers. We learned together. As a family.

And then Rowdy started rodeoing. Not casually. Seriously. High school rodeo. Team roping. Cutting, calf-roping, steer wrestling. Events that required skill and practice and showing up even when you didn't place. We traveled together. Camped at fairgrounds. Sat in the stands and watched him compete. And I saw him grow. Not just physically. But in confidence. In competence. In the quiet knowledge that he could do hard things.

He also started working with Ronnie and they slowly started taking a few small contracting jobs here and there. They took the jobs they wanted and they stayed close to home. We weren't getting back in the fast lane. We were restructuring life the way we wanted it. Slower. More connected.

Rowdy was learning construction. Contracting. How to build houses and barns and everything in between. By sixteen, Rowdy could frame, plumb, tile, sheetrock, roof, pour concrete. He could do work that most grown men can't do.

And he got serious about his music. Guitar. Singing. Writing songs. He had the time for it. Because he wasn't on a computer. Wasn't lost in screens. Wasn't being fed garbage by algorithms designed to make him anxious and insecure. He was with us. Working. Learning. Creating.

And as his mother, being there with him every single day, every step of the way, it was everything. We are extremely close because of it. Not just mother and son. But partners in this life. People who trust each other. Respect each other. Know each other deeply. That doesn't happen when you're running in different directions. It happens when you slow down. When you come home. When you choose presence over productivity.

Those years, were the quietest years of my adult life. And the most productive. Not in the way the world measures productivity. Not in revenue or achievements or things I could put on a resume. But in the things that actually matter. I healed. I grounded. I reconnected with God and the land and my family. I learned skills that will serve me for the rest of my life. I became whole again.

And when the Cowgirl Culture book was ready to launch in April 2024, when Bob Feist's Facebook post appeared in May, I was ready. Not because I'd been chasing the next thing. But because I'd been preparing without knowing what I was preparing for.

This is what rest looks like when you do it right. Not escaping. Not numbing. Not checking out. But slowing down enough to hear what's true. To heal what's broken. To build what matters. And to be ready when the next wave comes.

* * *

[THE LESSON]: Emotional Mastery Through Groundin\

You can't heal in the environment that made you sick. You have to remove yourself from the poison before you can detoxify. Whatever made you sick, quit the job, end the relationship, move to a different place, you can't heal while you're still there.

Grounding isn't metaphorical. It's literal. Bare feet on earth. Hands in soil. Sun on face. When you actually ground, your nervous system calms because your body remembers what peace feels like. Grounded people are harder to manipulate because their bodies know what's true.

Homesteading is resistance. When you can feed yourself, you can't be controlled. Self-sufficient people don't comply as easily, don't panic when supply chains break, don't trade freedom for safety.

Strong families don't need government intervention or permission to make decisions. When families work together and depend on each other, they become ungovernable.

Healing is returning to what's true. You're not broken, you're disconnected. When you reconnect and come home, healing happens naturally.

[YOUR TURN]

First: What environment is making you sick that you need to remove yourself from?

Second: How can you literally ground yourself, bare feet on earth, hands in soil, sun on face?

Third: What would self-sufficiency look like for you and your family?

____

____

____

____

____

____

<h1 style="text-align:center">15</h1>

Cowgirl Project

Back in 2016, I'd photographed 50 California cowgirls. I'd driven all over the state with that Dale Evans photo burned into my imagination, the inspiration that had started it all. Sharon Camarillo had given me my first ten names. Sandy Collier had been my first session. And each cowgirl had led me to the next, a chain of referrals that took me from the mountains to the ocean, from sprawling valley ranches to foothill properties overlooking the coast.

I stood where the first spade bit was forged. Saw collections of custom silver bits and trophy saddles that represented generations of mastery. I photographed women on legacy ranches, places that had been in families for over a century, passed down through generations, worked by the same bloodlines for longer than most businesses have existed. I saw some of the best horses you'd ever know. Animals bred for specific work, trained with patience and precision, worth more than most people's houses. I photographed women in traditional gear, handmade boots, custom hats, tack that told stories.

And I listened.

Every woman had something to teach me. Not just about ranching or horses or the Western way of life. But about resilience. About sacrifice. About what it takes to hold something together when the world is trying to tear it apart. These weren't the women you see on magazine covers. They weren't the ones with sponsorships and social media followings and carefully curated images. They were the ones doing the real work. Organizing work crews. Handling paperwork. Cooking meals. Raising kids. Keeping books. Roping. Riding. Doctoring cattle. Getting supplies on the ground before daylight. First up. Last to bed. Holding ranches together with muscle, instinct, and prayer.

Their hands were as rough as the men's. Their faces were sun-weathered and honest. Their stories were raw and real and worth preserving. One woman broke down in tears during her session. She was talking about her husband, the true love of her life. How she'd given up everything for that love. How it had been worth it. And then she paused. Looked me in the eye. And said: "Be smart. Make sure it's all in your name." Her daughter had lost two husbands over her horse passion. "I turned them out for my passion," she told me, unapologetic. And in that moment, I realized: this project wasn't about handmade boots or silver bits. It was about the deep soulfulness and salt-of-the-earth rawness and grit that cowgirls possess. The ability to love fiercely. And the courage to act on that love, even when it costs them everything.

I wanted to freeze time. Their faces. Their style. Their tack.

Their tools. Their land. Their culture. Before it was gone. Because Western culture is disappearing. Not dramatically. Not all at once. But slowly. Ranches getting sold to developers. Traditional skills being lost because younger generations don't have the time or patience to learn them. Stories dying with the people who lived them because nobody thought to write them down.

I wanted to stop that. Even if just for 50 women. Even if just in California. I wanted to create a record that would last. So their great-grandchildren could flip through pages someday and see their ancestor's strength, beauty, and spirit. So people who'd never set foot on a ranch could understand what it takes to live this life. So the world would remember: cowgirls aren't just a costume. They're a culture.

And then I shelved the project.

Because I bought HERLIFE Magazine. And suddenly I didn't have time for passion projects that didn't generate revenue. I was running a magazine. The Cowgirl Culture photos sat in a folder on my hard drive. Waiting. For years.

During those years, the women would reach out. "When's the book coming?" "I'm so excited to see it." "My friends keep asking." And I'd tell them: "Soon. I promise. I'm working on it." But I wasn't. Because I didn't have the bandwidth. The time. The energy. The project was alive, but dormant. Waiting for me to be ready.

When I sold HERLIFE in early 2022, the first thing I did was open that folder. I looked at the images I'd taken six years earlier. And I felt something I hadn't felt in a long time. Not obligation. Not guilt. Excitement. These women had been patient. They'd waited. They'd believed in me even when I couldn't deliver. And now I could finally give them what I'd promised.

I reached out to the women I'd already photographed. Some had moved. Some had aged. Some had lost loved ones or sold ranches or changed directions. But they all remembered.

Here's what nobody tells you about publishing a book, especially a photography book with custom layouts and design: It's overwhelming. Not the photography part. I knew how to do that. But the publishing part? That was entirely new territory. ISBN registration, copyright law, how to format a book for print, how to work with printers, how to create a layout that flows, how to price it, how to market it, how to build a website to sell it, how to handle distribution, how to manage inventory. Every single piece. Similar but different.

And the hardest part? Just getting started. I offer this now in my courses as well. Are thinking about publishing a book?

Most people never finish projects because they're waiting for perfection. They're waiting to know exactly how it's going to turn out before they start. They're waiting for the perfect layout, the perfect design, the perfect everything. And while they're waiting, the project dies. Because perfection is the enemy of done.

Start ugly. That's the lesson. Start messy. Start imperfect. Start before you know what you're doing. Because you can fix ugly. You can refine messy. You can improve imperfect. But you can't finish what you never start.

So I started ugly. I opened a blank InDesign file and started dropping in photos. No plan. No perfect vision. Just: put something on the page. And it was terrible. The layouts were clunky. The spacing was off. The flow didn't work. But it was something. And something is better than nothing.

So I kept going. Day after day. Adding photos. Writing captions. Adjusting layouts. Moving things around. Deleting sections that didn't work. Starting over when I had to.

Eight months. That's how long it took on the publishing side alone. Eight months of learning. Testing. Revising. Troubleshooting. Eight months of late nights and frustration and moments where I thought, this is too hard. I should just hire someone.

But I didn't. Because I wanted to own the entire process. I wanted to know that if I ever did this again, for myself or for someone else, I could do it from start to finish without relying on anyone. That's mastery. Not hiring experts to do it for you. But learning it so deeply that you become the expert.

In April 2024, Cowgirl Culture: California launched. The book was everything I'd envisioned eight years earlier. Full-color photography. Stories that honored these women. Layouts that felt professional and polished. A physical artifact that would last. Not a magazine that gets recycled after a month. But a book that sits on coffee tables. Gets passed down. Becomes part of the legacy.

I announced it online. Through social media. Directly to the cowgirls who were featured. And the response was overwhelming. Women reaching out saying: "This is what we needed." "This is our story." "Thank you for telling it." "My daughter cried when she saw my spread." "My granddaughter wants to be a cowgirl now." These weren't just nice comments. They were proof that the work mattered. That stopping time, preserving these women's faces and stories and culture, was worth the eight-year wait.

I felt something when that book launched that I hadn't felt in years. Pure creative satisfaction. Not success measured in revenue or client count or how many copies sold. But the deep, soul-level satisfaction of creating something that honored people I respected. Something that preserved a culture I loved. Something that would outlive me.

Here's what that book taught me: Some projects are worth waiting for. If I'd rushed it in 2016, if I'd tried to publish it while running HERLIFE, while stretched thin, while not fully present, it wouldn't have been as good. The writing would have been weaker. The layouts less thoughtful. The execution rushed. But because I waited. Because I let it sit and mature. Because I came back to it with fresh eyes and more experience, it was better. Not everything needs to be done immediately. Some projects need to rest. To wait for you to be ready. To simmer until the timing is right. And when you return to them, with more skill, more wisdom, more clarity, you build something stronger than you could have built the first time.

The Cowgirl Culture book restored something in me. After selling HERLIFE, after bending the knee, after losing my voice for a paycheck, I needed to create something that was purely mine. Something nobody could tell me to soften. Something nobody could demand I change. Something that didn't require compromise.

The cowgirls gave me that. They trusted me with their stories. They let me into their lives. They believed I would honor them. And I did. Not perfectly. But honestly. And that mattered more.

Looking back, I can see how everything connected. The photography skills I'd built over decades. The publishing knowledge I'd gained at HERLIFE. The writing lessons Marilyn taught me. The design principles I'd absorbed. All of it came together in that book. This is what mastery looks like. Not one skill in isolation. But many skills woven together to create something larger than any single piece. Photography plus writing plus design plus publishing plus marketing equals a book that matters.

And now I can teach it. Not just "here's how to take a good photo." But "here's how to turn your vision into a published artifact that preserves culture and tells stories and creates legacy." That's what Magazine Mastery is built on. The real, practical, proven process of going from idea to published work. You can do it and I'm here for you if you're ready.

* * *

[THE LESSON]: Start Ugly, Finish Strong

Perfection is the enemy of done. Get paint on the canvas. Most people never finish because they're waiting for perfection. While they wait, the project dies. Start ugly, messy, imperfect. You can fix ugly, but you can't finish what you never start.

Some projects plant themselves and wait for you. In 2016, I photographed 50 cowgirls but wasn't ready to finish. The project waited six years. When I returned in 2022 with more experience, I built something better. Not every project needs to be finished immediately. Some need to rest, mature, wait for you to grow into them.

Legacy work requires patience. The Cowgirl Culture book will outlast me. That's legacy work: creating something that preserves culture, honors people, tells truth.

You don't need permission to preserve culture. Nobody hired me. I just decided it mattered.

Teaching what you learn multiplies the impact. One book preserves 50 stories. Teaching 100 people preserves 5,000 stories.

[YOUR TURN]

First: What project are you waiting to perfect instead of starting?

Second: What bones have you already laid down that are waiting for you to return?

Third: What culture or stories do you need to preserve?

16

Roping Bible

I was wrapping up the final details on the Cowgirl Culture book when I saw the post. May 2024. Scrolling through Facebook. And there it was: Bob Feist was retiring. Ropers Sports News, the 58-year-old publication that had been documenting team roping and rodeo since 1968, was closing its doors. To most people, that was just another post. Another business closing. Another piece of nostalgia fading away. But to me? It hit like a freight train.

I knew that publication. I'd known it my entire life. When I was a teenager, working at my grandmother's western wear store in Lodi, Bob Feist used to come in. He'd pull up in his truck. Walk in with stacks of newspapers, thick, newsprint publications packed with results, statistics, upcoming events, stories from the roping world. Ropers Sports News. He'd set them on the counter. Exchange a few words with whoever was working. And head out to the next stop.

I didn't know then that I was watching a legend. I didn't know that Bob Feist was one of the first people to ever create a rodeo and roping publication. I didn't know he was a world-renowned roper himself. A commentator. A promoter who'd been building the sport since the 1960s. I didn't know that the newspapers he was dropping on our counter would come to be called "The Roping Bible," the original, the first of its kind. The publication that every serious team roper read. The one that held the history of the sport in its pages. I was just a kid. He was just a man delivering papers. But I remembered him.

And now, decades later, I was reading that he was closing it down. Fifty-eight years of history. Fifty-eight years of documenting team roping, rodeo, Western sports. Archives full of stories, results, photos that would be lost if the publication just disappeared. And I thought: I can't let this die.

Not maybe I could save it. Not possibly I could run it. I knew I could. I'd just spent years running HERLIFE Magazine. I'd learned publishing from the ground up, editorial, design, sales, operations, printing, distribution. I'd just spent eight months teaching myself how to publish a book from scratch. I knew how to take a publication and make it better. And more importantly: I cared. This wasn't just a business opportunity. This was preserving history. Honoring legacy. Keeping alive something that mattered to a community I was part of.

I called Sharon again. Sharon and I had become close during the Cowgirl Culture project. She'd opened doors for me. Introduced me to women I needed to meet. Trusted me with stories. She was my neighbor. My friend. And she knew Bob.

"Sharon," I said, "I saw Bob's post. About closing Ropers Sports News."

"Yeah," she said quietly. "End of an era."

"Do you think he'd sell it?"

Pause. "You're serious?"

"Dead serious. Will you connect me with him? See if he'll meet with me?"

She didn't hesitate. "I'll call him."

A week later, I was sitting across from Bob Feist at the Velvet Grill in Galt, California. Two publishers. Two generations. One legacy on the table. I'd brought my work. Past copies of HERLIFE Magazine. The Cowgirl Culture book, fresh off the press and still smelling like ink. I wanted him to see proof. Not just words. Not just promises. But evidence that I knew what I was doing. That I could handle what he'd built.

We ordered food. Made small talk. And then I laid it out.

"Bob, I want to buy Ropers Sports News. I know you've built something incredible over fifty-eight years. I know it's your legacy. And I know you wouldn't sell it to just anyone."

He listened. Said nothing. Just watched me with those sharp, assessing eyes.

"I'm not interested in letting it die," I continued. "I want to transform it. Take it from a newspaper format to a glossy magazine. Modernize the design. Expand the content. Grow the readership."

I slid the Cowgirl Culture book across the table.

"But I also want to preserve what you've built. The history. The integrity. The reputation. This isn't just a business acquisition for me. This is honoring fifty-eight years of work. This is keeping The Roping Bible alive."

Bob picked up the book. Flipped through it slowly. Studied the layouts. The photography. The quality. Then he looked at the HERLIFE issues. Page by page. Taking his time. And then he set them down and looked at me.

"You know," he said, "I've had other people interested. Team ropers who think they can run a publication because they love the sport. But they don't know anything about publishing. They don't understand what it takes." He tapped the Cowgirl Culture book. "You have what it takes."

We closed the deal in June 2024. One month after I saw his Facebook post. I became the owner of Ropers Sports News, the 58-year-old publication that had been documenting Western sports since before I was born. The publication I'd watched Bob deliver to my grandmother's store when I was a teenager. The publication that held the history of a sport and a culture I'd grown up in. And now it was my responsibility.

Here's the thing nobody tells you about buying a legacy: It's not like buying a new business where you can just blow it up and start over. It's like adopting someone's child. Bob had built Ropers Sports News from nothing. He'd poured decades of his life into it. He'd documented champions, covered events, created a resource that the entire roping community relied on. And he was trusting me to keep it alive. That's not just responsibility. That's sacred trust. I couldn't just change everything and hope for the best. I had to honor what he'd built while also bringing it into the modern era. I had to prove I belonged, not just because Bob chose me, but because I could actually do the work.

And I was walking into the good old boys' club of Western sports. A world where women were often decorative. Not decision-makers. A world where tradition mattered more than innovation. Where "we've always done it this way" was the answer to every question. A world that didn't necessarily want a woman publisher telling them how things were going to change.

The resistance started immediately. "We do it this way." "It's always been done like this." "Bob never did that." "Who do you think you are, young lady?"

That last one. That phrase. Who do you think you are? It's the question designed to make you second-guess yourself. To make you feel like you're overstepping. To remind you that you're an outsider. That you need to stay small. The omega to the alpha.

And then the phone call came.

One of the longtime advertisers, a man who'd been placing ads with Ropers Sports News for years, called me directly. His voice was tight. Controlled. But I could hear the anger underneath it.

"I need to talk to you about the direction you're taking this paper," he said.

"I'm listening."

"This is not a women's magazine. This has never been a women's magazine. And I don't know who you think you are, young lady, but you're not going to come in here and change it. We don't want women on the covers. We don't want all this women's content. This is a roping publication. It's always been about the men. The real ropers."

I was on the highway 15 driving to the National Finals Rodeo in Las Vegas, he was coming through the speakers of my whip, my hair stood up on my neck, and I felt something shift inside me. My voice found a lower tone, a steady baritone.

I'd been here before. I'd stood in this exact moment before. Different publication. Different advertiser. Same demand: silence yourself. Make your voice smaller. Edit your values to fit someone else's comfort. That hospital executive while at HERLIFE, sitting across from me in her mask, telling me she was "in the business of selling COVID." I'd bent the knee that day. I'd apologized for something I wasn't sorry for. I'd sold my voice for a contract. And it had crushed my soul. It had crushed my creativity. It had broken something inside me that took years to rebuild.

I wasn't going to do that again.

"Let me be clear about something," I said, steadily. "I appreciate your years of support with this publication. I respect the history you have with Bob and with Ropers Sports News. But I am not going to stop featuring women and Im not shifting my editorial schedule because you're uncomfortable."

Silence on the other end.

"Here's what I see," I continued. "I see a wave coming. Women athletes in rodeo are growing. Breakaway roping. Barrel racing. Team roping. Women are competing at higher levels than ever before. They're buying horses. They're buying tack. They're spending money in this industry. And nobody is talking to them. Nobody is putting them on covers. Nobody is telling their stories. I'm going to change that. Not because it's politically correct. Because it's smart business. Because there's an entire audience that's been ignored, and I'm going to be the one who speaks to them, and if your too short-sided to see the opportunity than we are probably not a fit for one another."

I could hear him breathing on the other end. Processing.

"You can keep your advertising dollars," I said. "I'd rather have my integrity and my vision than your money. "

He hung up without another word.

I was infuriated. I was fearful too. What was he going to say about me. How would the good 'ol boys take me rising up against the machine. My mind was busy after that. For many days. After a couple hours of fear, I dropped that shit like a bad habit and stood behind my decision. Finally in the power of trusting my instincts. Of believing in my vision even when someone was demanding I shrink it. This wasn't HERLIFE. This time, I wasn't going to waver. This time, I wasn't going to bend the knee. This time, I was going to bet on myself.

The people who ask "Who do you think you are?" are the ones who are most threatened by the answer. Because if you actually know who you are, if you're confident in your value, your skills, your vision, their question has no power. So I answered it. Every time. Not defensively. Not apologetically. But clearly. No distortion-pure tone. Like ringing a bell.

"I'm the publisher of Ropers Sports News. I'm the person Bob Feist chose to carry on his legacy. I'm going to feature women athletes because they deserve to be seen. And I'm here to make this publication better while honoring everything he built."

And then I kept working.

Here's what I knew that they didn't: You can't create from competition. And it's one of the most important lessons in business. Most people approach new opportunities from a competitive mindset. They think: How do I beat what came before? How do I prove I'm better? How do I show everyone they were wrong? But that mindset kills creativity. Because you're not creating something new. You're just reacting to what already exists.

I wasn't competing with Bob Feist's legacy. I was honoring it. I wasn't trying to prove his way was wrong. I was trying to build on what he'd started. I wasn't fighting against the old guard. I was inviting them into a new vision that still respected where they came from.

That's the difference between creating from competition and creating from collaboration. Competition says: "My way is better than your way." Collaboration says: "What you built was incredible. Now let's see what we can build together." And when you approach legacy work from that place, from respect instead of rivalry, people feel it. Not everyone. Some will resist no matter what. But the right people? They lean in.

I also knew: Money is a value metric. When I made my offer to Bob, I didn't lowball him. I didn't try to steal his legacy for pennies. I made a fair offer. An offer that honored what he'd built. An offer that said: "I know what this is worth." Because how you pay for something reflects how you value it. If I'd tried to get Ropers Sports News for cheap, Bob would have known I didn't truly value what he'd created. But because I paid fairly, he knew I understood. I respected the work. I honored the legacy. And that mattered more than the transaction itself.

This is what people miss about money: It's not just currency. It's communication. How you handle money tells people what you value. What you respect. What you're willing to invest in. And when you approach transactions with integrity, when you pay fairly, honor commitments, treat money as a reflection of value, people trust you.

By the time I'm writing this, I've published ten issues of Ropers Sports News. And the publication is changing. Not radically. Not overnight. But steadily. We're attracting new readers. Younger readers. Women readers. People who love the sport but had given up on the publication because it felt outdated. We're modernizing the design. Expanding the content. Bringing in fresh voices while still covering the traditional results and events that the core audience expects.

We're building while honoring. Innovating while respecting. Moving forward while staying rooted.

And the women? They're on the covers now. Their stories are being told. The wave I saw coming? It's here. And I caught it because I refused to let someone else's discomfort dictate my vision.

The resistance is still there. There are still people who don't like change. Who preferred the old newspaper format. Who think a woman has no business running The Roping Bible. But there are also people who are thrilled. Who've been waiting for this publication to evolve. Who are excited to see what's next. The people who align with the vision are finding us. And the people who don't? They're naturally falling away.

That's how it works. You can't please everyone. And trying to do so just dilutes your vision. So I stopped trying. I stopped worrying about the critics. Stopped defending every decision. Stopped explaining myself to people who were never going to support me anyway. And I focused on the work. On serving the readers who want what we're building. On honoring Bob's legacy by making it relevant for a new generation. On creating something that will last another 58 years.

Here's my vision for Ropers Sports News: Right now, we publish six issues a year. Eventually, we'll grow to ten. Right now, each issue is about 60-80 pages. Eventually, they'll be 100-150 pages. We're going to expand distribution. Grow the subscriber base. Bring in more advertisers who want to reach the roping community.

But more than that, I want to preserve Western culture the way I did with 'Cowgirl Culture.' I want to start the 'Western Elders Series.' A project where I photograph and interview the elders of our Western world, ropers, ranchers, cowboys, cowgirls who have lived this life for decades and carry stories that need to be preserved. Their struggles. Their triumphs. Their wisdom. I want to freeze time. To document their faces, their hands, their tools, their land before they're gone. Not just in the magazine. But in books. In archives. In permanent records that will outlast all of us. Because legacy work isn't just about running a business. It's about preserving culture. And that's what I'm building here. Not just a magazine. But a record of a way of life that's disappearing.

I also want to help other people tell their stories. I'm evolving into a publisher, not just of my own work, but of others' work too. Through my Publishing Mastery courses, I'm teaching people how to: start their own magazines, publish their own books, document the cultures they care about, build businesses around storytelling. Because if I can do it, they can too. And the more people who know how to preserve culture, document history, and tell stories, the less we lose.

Looking back, I can see how everything led here. The Cowgirl Culture project taught me how to honor culture with respect and authenticity. HERLIFE taught me how to run a publication, manage advertisers, build systems, navigate the business side. Selling HERLIFE taught me what happens when you compromise your voice, and why I'd never do it again. The quiet years after HERLIFE taught me how to rest, study, prepare for the next wave without forcing it. And Bob Feist's Facebook post? That was the wave I'd been preparing to catch. I just didn't know it yet.

Find all of this in my educational courses. Not just how to build a business. But why some opportunities are worth taking and others aren't. How to recognize the difference between chasing success and building legacy. How to prepare for opportunities you can't see coming yet. How to take something someone else built and make it yours while still honoring their vision. How to walk into rooms where you're not wanted and prove you belong anyway. Not by being loud. Not by fighting. But by doing the work so well that they can't deny your value.

That's what Ropers Sports News is teaching me every day. How to hold my ground when people say "Who do you think you are?" How to honor legacy while building the future. How to stay true to my vision even when the old guard resists. How to build something that matters more than money. And how to write my own story, even when someone else started the book.

* * *

[THE LESSON]: You Belong Where Your Value Is

Real relationships create opportunities you can't strategize. Sharon connected me to Bob because we'd built genuine trust. You can't fake authenticity or manipulate people into opening doors. When you show up with integrity and honor people, they open doors you didn't even know existed.

You can't create from competition. Competition asks "How do I beat what came before?" Creation asks "How do I honor what came before while building what comes next?" When you approach legacy work from collaboration, honoring the foundation while building new floors, you create something that lasts.

Money is a value metric. How you pay for something reflects how you value it. Fair offers communicate respect.

"Who do you think you are?" is a test. If you know the answer clearly and confidently, the question loses its power.

Never bend the knee twice. If you've learned what happens when you silence yourself for money, trust that lesson. Stand tall. Bet on your vision. The right people will find you.

Do the work so well they can't deny your value. Build for the people who believe, not the people who resist.

[YOUR TURN]

First: What legacy are you being called to carry forward?

____

____

____

____

____

Second: How do you answer "Who do you think you are?"

____

____

____

Third: Where have you been asked to make yourself smaller? What would standing tall look like?

17

On the Road

The thing about buying a legacy publication is this: You can't just sit in an office and run it. You have to show up. You have to be present. You have to meet the people whose stories you're telling.

So since June 2024, I've been on the road. A lot.

I've covered ropings all over the West. California, Nevada, Arizona. Big events. Small jackpots. Everything in between. I've been to Circle N Arena in Tulare, California, Fillmore Roping Club, Chowchilla Western Stampede, Rancho Rio in Wickenburg, Arizona, Dynamite Arena, Horns & Hooves Arena, Western Trails Ranch, The National Finals Rodeo in Las Vegas, The World Series of Team Roping Finale at South Point, ACTRA Finals in Reno, Patriot Events during NFR week, National Finals Breakaway Roping, dozens of weekly jackpots and smaller ropings.

I've met producers. Ropers. Sponsors. Advertisers. Photographers. Announcers. Stock contractors. I've stood in arenas at 6 AM watching practice runs. I've stayed until midnight photographing the last go-round. I've distributed magazines. Shaken hands. Introduced myself a hundred times: "Hi, I'm Dee Yates, the new publisher of Ropers Sports News."

And every single time, I've watched their reaction.

Some people are thrilled. They love what I'm doing with the publication. They're excited about the direction. They want to support it. Some people are cautious. They liked the old format. They're not sure about change. They want to see if I can actually pull this off before they commit. And some people? Some people are cold. Not rude, exactly. Just distant. Dismissive. Like they're waiting for me to fail so they can say "I told you so."

God bless the newspaper business. And God bless what Ropers Sports News has always been. I absolutely love it and admire it. But getting in there was like climbing into a clunky old Datsun pickup and trying to roll down the fast lane. I had great intentions of making that publication into a high gloss magazine. And I jumped in the Datsun pickup and took off down the highway and it was hard trying to find a gear while dealing with the old boys' club that Bob Feist had developed over 58 years.

This is the good old boys' club I talked about in the last chapter. But it's not just men.

Here's what nobody talks about: The bitch club is real too.

Not all women. Not even most women. But there are a few, particularly in Western media, who have been nothing but cold to me from day one. Women who won't speak to me. Won't engage. Won't return emails or calls. Women who have no reason to be hostile. I most of them I've never even formally met. But they're threatened. Because I'm building something. Because I'm creating. Because I'm working hard and gaining traction. And instead of celebrating that, instead of seeing another woman succeed and thinking "Good for her, that's possible for me too," they see it as competition.

They think there's not enough for everybody. And so they ice me out. They pretend I don't exist. They make subtle digs in conversations with mutual contacts.

It's fascinating, honestly. Because here's what I know: You never know who you're going to need someday. You never know who you'll want to collaborate with. Who'll open a door for you. Who'll have information or connections that could help you. So be good to everyone. All the time. Not because you're fake. Not because you're trying to manipulate. But because kindness and generosity create opportunities. And jealousy creates lag.

Here's what I want to say to anyone reading this who's struggling with jealousy: Check it. Seriously. It's a waste of your time. It's a waste of your energy. And it's actively working against you. Because you are what you think about. If you spend your time resenting other people's success, you're manifesting lack. You're telling the universe: "There's not enough. I'm threatened. I have to protect what's mine." But if you celebrate other people's wins, if you genuinely feel happy when someone else succeeds, you're manifesting abundance. You're saying: "There's plenty. Success is possible. If they can do it, so can I."

Jealousy doesn't protect you. It limits you. And the women who've been cold to me? They're not hurting me. They're hurting themselves. Because while they're busy being threatened, I'm building relationships with everyone else. I'm creating opportunities. I'm moving forward. And eventually, they'll need something I have. Or know someone I know. Or want to collaborate on something. And I'll remember how they treated me. Not with revenge. Not with pettiness. But with clarity about who's actually on my team and who's just protecting their turf.

Most of the people I've met on the road have been incredible. Generous. Supportive. Excited about what I'm building.

Like Chris Neal, who runs the Patriot Events. He stepped up during NFR week and created amazing competitions for juniors and ladies. His Rope for the Crown event was phenomenal. Like Ty Yost, who runs events in Wickenburg and has built an empire around team roping. His Title Fights drew massive crowds, the kind of attendance that proves this sport is growing, not shrinking. Like the producers at ACTRA who welcomed me to their finals in Reno and made me feel like part of the family. Like Tracy Hammond, who interviewed me for her show Wild Ride TV on the Cowboy Channel and gave Ropers Sports News incredible exposure. Like the "underground girl gang," the women who've quietly supported me, connected me with people, cheered me on from behind the scenes.

These are my people. Not the ones who are threatened. But the ones who see what I'm building and say: "How can I help?"

In February 2025, I took one of the most important trips of my publishing career. Arizona. Specifically, Wickenburg, the team roping capital of the world in winter months. I packed up the truck and trailer. Loaded my camera gear. Brought my homeschool curriculum. And I took Rowdy with me.

For a month, we lived on the road. Homeschool in the pickup between ropings. Rowdy competing in events. Me photographing, distributing magazines, meeting producers, building relationships. It was chaos. It was exhausting. It was one of the best months of my life.

Because I got to watch my son experience the sport he loves while I documented it. I got to work alongside him instead of away from him. And I got to see firsthand what Arizona's roping community is like.

Wickenburg in February is unreal. If you love team roping, it's Disneyland. There are ropings happening every single day. Multiple arenas. Multiple producers. Jackpots, championships, qualifiers, fun ropings, serious ropings, ropings for every level and skill. I covered weekly jackpots where 60+ teams would show up on a random Thursday.

The energy was electric. And the landscape? Stunning. The

desert. The mountains. The saguaros standing tall against sunsets that looked like paintings. Arizona is different from California. The ranches are different. The terrain is different. The culture has its own flavor. But the cowgirls? Just as strong. Just as dedicated. Just as worth documenting.

During that month, I photographed 35 Arizona cowgirls for my second book: Cowgirl Culture: Arizona, Vol II. I drove all over the state. Met women on working ranches. In cutting horse facilities. At barrel racing arenas. Women who run cattle operations. Who train horses. Who compete at the highest levels while raising families and running businesses. Women whose stories deserve to be preserved.

And just like with the California book, I was struck by how different each woman's story was, yet how similar the spirit. Grit. Resilience. Love for the land. Love for the animals. Love for the life. These women aren't performing cowgirl. They're living it. And I'm honored to document it.

But while I was photographing cowgirls and covering ropings, something was weighing on me.

We're losing the elders.

Every event I attend, I see them. The men and women in their 70s, 80s, 90s who've been in this sport for decades. The ones who built it. Who remember when team roping was just a few guys in a pasture, not a multi-million-dollar industry. The ones who know the history. The techniques. The stories that will die with them if we don't write them down.

And they're aging out. Passing away. Taking their knowledge with them. I see it happening in real time. At NFR week, I watched an 87-year-old roper compete. Still sharp. Still skilled. But how many more years does he have? At ACTRA Finals, I met a woman who'd been roping for 60 years. She remembered when there were no women's divisions. When she had to fight just to be allowed in the arena. Her stories were gold. And she might not be here next year to tell them.

This is urgent.

I have a vision, a project where I photograph and interview the elders of our Western world. Not just ropers. But ranchers. Cowboys. Cowgirls. People who've lived this life for 50, 60, 70 years and carry wisdom we can't afford to lose. I want to document their faces, the lines that tell stories of sun and wind and hard work. Their hands, calloused, scarred, capable. Their tools, the saddles and ropes and bits that have been with them for decades. Their land, the places they've worked and loved and fought to keep. Their stories, the triumphs, the failures, the lessons they learned the hard way.

I want to freeze time before it's too late. Because once they're gone, those stories are gone. And we'll have lost something we can never get back.

This is the work that drives me now. Not just running Ropers Sports News. Not just publishing magazines. But preserving culture. Because Western culture is disappearing. Not dramatically. Not all at once. But slowly, steadily, as the people who lived it die and the younger generation forgets.

Ranches get sold to developers. Skills get lost because nobody taught them. Stories die untold. And if we don't document it, if we don't photograph it, write it down, record it, it's gone forever.

That's what I'm fighting for. Every event I cover for Ropers Sports News is part of this work. Every cowgirl I photograph for Cowgirl Culture is part of the work. Every elder I interview for the Western Elders Series will be part of it too. I'm not just building a business. I'm building a record. A permanent, physical, lasting record of a way of life that matters.

And it's exhausting. And it's expensive. And it takes me away from home more than I'd like. But it's worth it.

Because 50 years from now, when someone opens one of my books or flips through an old issue of Ropers Sports News, they'll see what this world looked like. They'll see the faces of the people who lived it. They'll read the stories of what it took to survive and thrive in this life. And they'll know: This mattered. These people mattered. This culture was worth preserving.

The road is hard. I've driven 16 hours straight to make it to an event. I've missed Rowdy's rodeos because I was covering someone else's. I've dealt with the good old boys' club telling me I don't know what I'm doing. I've dealt with the bitch club freezing me out because they're threatened. I've dealt with exhaustion and loneliness and moments where I wondered if it was worth it.

But then I show up at an arena. And a roper comes up to me and says: "I've been reading Ropers Sports News since I was a kid. Thank you for keeping it alive." Or a cowgirl sees her photo in Cowgirl Culture and cries because someone finally saw her. Really saw her. Or an elder tells me a story I've never heard before and says: "I'm so glad someone's writing this down."

And I remember why I'm doing this. Not for money. Not for recognition. Not for applause. For legacy. For the record. For the people whose stories deserve to be told.

This is the work I was made to do. Not just publishing. Not just photography. But preservation. Documenting culture before it's lost. Honoring people while they're still here to be honored. Creating artifacts that will outlast all of us.

And I'm just getting started.

* * *

[THE LESSON]: Do the Work That Outlasts You

Jealousy is wasted energy. While they're busy being jealous, you're building relationships, creating opportunities, moving forward. When you celebrate others' wins, you're manifesting abundance. Check your jealousy. It's creating lag in your life.

Be good to everyone. You never know who you'll need

someday. You never know whose door will open for you.

Show up. Be present. Do the work. You can't build legacy from a distance. You have to meet the people whose stories you're telling.

Document the elders before it's too late. Every day, another elder passes away. Another story is lost. If you care about preserving culture, act now. Interview them. Photograph them. Record their stories.

Legacy work is hard. Do it anyway. The road is exhausting, but 50 years from now, nobody will remember how tired you were. They'll remember the work you created. The stories you told. The culture you preserved. That's what lasts.

[YOUR TURN]

First: What jealousy are you holding onto that's creating lag in your life?

____

____

____

____

____

Second: Who are the elders in your world whose stories need to be documented before it's too late?

Third: What legacy work are you avoiding because it's hard?

18

And Then He Died

A few weeks before my father died, I went over to his house. He was becoming immobile. Complaining about his foot hurting because of the neuropathy. He was just sitting there in his house, not moving, and his mind was starting to leave him. It made things complicated, trying to talk to him. Trying to reason with him.

I made him go outside and sit in the sun.

"You need to get up," I told him. "You need to move. You need to walk."

He argued with me. Fought with me. Told me I didn't understand, that it was too painful.

"You need to get up and walk before you can't walk anymore."

He told me I was crazy. That I didn't know what I was talking about.

But I knew. Cognitively, I knew he wasn't thinking right. And I was so scared. His foot was so swollen. He had a big sore on it. I was terrified that if he didn't grab ahold of himself and become mobile, he was never going to walk again.

Fighting and arguing between him and me was not uncommon. We were both stubborn. Both fighters. But this was different. This was me watching my father slip away and not knowing how to stop it.

I screamed at him: "God dammit, you need to get up and fight! You're the one that taught me how to fight! You need to get up and fight! Fight for yourself! Fight for your life! You're slipping away!"

He sat there quietly. His head sunk down. His sunglasses on. The sun hitting his face. He didn't say anything.

I grabbed him. I hugged him. I told him I loved him. I told him I didn't want to see him quit fighting.

And then I went off to a rodeo.

Weeks later, I got the phone call from my mom. My dad was down. He was sick. Unresponsive. He had been unresponsive all day and my mom didn't know what to do.

I got to my mom's house as fast as I could. He was laying on the bed.

I laid down next to him. "Daddy, can you hear me?"

He looked up at me. "Yeah."

"Daddy, you're sick. I need to take you in."

"No. I'm not going."

"I'm taking you and you're gonna be nice."

I held his hands. Rowdy came in and we got sweats on him. My son, this young man my father had poured his life into, scooped his grandfather up and carried him to the car. We loaded up and drove him to town. I was in the driver's seat and he was in the passenger seat. Mom, Rowdy, and Ronnie in the backseat.

I looked over at him. He had his sweatshirt on and his seat belt on, and his head was hanging. I held him with my hand across his chest, right over his heart. I called to him.

"Daddy, can you hear me?"

"Yes, I hear you."

"Do you know where we're going?"

"Yes. We're going to the hospital."

And then he said something I will carry with me forever. His voice was weak, but clear.

"I just want you to know, Dee. I never quit fighting. I was

always fighting."

I held him tighter, my hand on his heart, tears streaming down my face. He heard me that day in the sun. He heard me screaming at him to fight. And he wanted me to know: he never stopped.

"Yeah, we're going to the hospital. Daddy, I love you. Hang on."

We drove to the hospital. Took him in. And that was the last time I ever talked to him.

It crushed me. And then everything stopped.

August 5, 2025. Donald Russell Meidinger. Born December 1952 in Victor, California. He was 72 years old.

My dad. The man who taught me to be tough, to be strong, to ball up my fist and never back down. The man whose pride was both a gift and a burden. The man I couldn't have become who I am without. And the man who loved me more than anything in this world.

Our relationship was complex. It could fill its own book, and maybe someday it will. But here it is: my father was hard on me. He was hard on all of us. He was hard on himself. I believe he taught us how to be tough by being hard, knowing that this world is full of hard work and sacrifice. He wanted us to survive. More than that, he wanted us to thrive.

He was the man who told me I'd never make money taking pictures. The man who went silent for weeks, sometimes months, when I made big decisions he didn't approve of. Every major move I made in my life followed the same pattern: I'd announce something, he'd go quiet. Not angry quiet. Worried quiet. The silence of a man who grew up dirt poor, who knew what it meant to lose everything, who was terrified his daughter would end up the same way.

When I bought my first property in Valley Springs, he went silent. But then he helped me build it.

When I bought the property in Lodi, he went silent. But then he came and saw what I'd created.

When I started businesses, took risks, built things he didn't understand, he'd go silent. And then he'd show up.

That was the pattern. Silence, then presence. Doubt, then support. Fear, then pride.

And through all of it, through every silent treatment and every worried look and every time he shook his head at my decisions, I always knew one thing: he was right there. Right behind me. Even when I couldn't see him. Even when I couldn't hear him. I knew that if I fell, he would be there to catch me. That knowledge, that certainty, was the foundation I built everything on. He might not say the words. He might go weeks without calling. But if I needed him, truly needed him, he would show up. He always did.

But Ropers Sports News was different.

When I told my father I was going to buy a 58-year-old roping publication, something shifted. Maybe it was because he was getting older, getting sicker. Maybe it was because he'd watched me prove myself so many times that the doubt had finally worn away. Maybe it was because this was a legacy publication, something that connected to the Western world he loved. I don't know. But for the first time in my life, my father didn't go silent.

He said yes.

Not just yes. He said: "I have absolutely no doubt in you. I know you can do this. You've proven yourself time and time again. Go for it. Jump. I know you'll make it happen."

I stood there, choked up. I couldn't speak. The words were stuck in my throat. This was the moment I'd been waiting for my entire life. Full, unconditional approval. No hesitation. No worry. No silence. Just belief.

"I know you'll work it," he said. "I've been amazed by everything you've done. I know without a shadow of doubt you will be successful."

He put his golden seal on it. His blessing. His complete and total support.

And then he did something I'd never seen him do before. He went to a sign shop and had my logo made, the Ropers Sports

News logo, and he plastered them on the side of his truck. On his trailer. On anything that would hold them. My father, this proud man who'd spent decades building his own name, drove around town advertising his daughter's business. Because he was proud of me. Not quietly proud. Not eventually proud. Loudly, visibly, drive-it-down-the-street proud.

That was the full circle moment. The little girl who'd been told she'd never make money taking pictures. The woman who'd rebuilt from collapse, who'd run magazines, and flipped properties, developed systems and businessses, who'd photographed a thousand of people and written hundreds of stories. That woman finally had her father's complete approval. And it meant everything.

From the day I bought Ropers Sports News until the day he died, we spoke every single day about that business. Every day. He helped gave me advise on everything. I didn't need any of it, but I wanted all of it; I knew the time was becoming short. We'd sit together and talk about what I was building, what I was changing, what I was learning. There was no arguing. No silence. No doubt. Just two people, father and daughter, building something together.

It was the one project, the last project, that he was completely there for. Completely present. Completely supportive. And I will carry that with me forever.

The days before he died were the hardest of my life. He was on life support. Diabetes. Heart failure. A leg amputation. A stroke. We had to make a decision. My mother Vickie, who had cared for him through everything, who never left his side, who loved him fiercely for almost 50 years, looked at me. And I screamed. Aloud. In that hospital room.

"That's it? We just take him off life support? That's it? We're done? We just walk away? I don't know how to do this."

I didn't know how to let him go. I didn't know how to say goodbye to the man who had been right behind me my entire life. Even when he doubted my decisions. Even when he disapproved. Even when he went silent. He was always there.

And suddenly, he wasn't.

The overwhelming feeling I had in that moment, and for weeks after, was free falling. Like the ground had dropped out from under me. Like I was falling and falling and there was nothing to catch me. My father had always been my safety net, even when I didn't realize it. And now he was gone, and I was in a tailspin. A loneliness so deep it felt like drowning. A sadness that swallowed everything.

Our family became very lonely. Very sad. With his absence. Because my dad wasn't just my dad. He was the center. The one who held us together even when things were broken. And without him, I didn't know how to be.

I wrote and delivered his eulogy. I stood in front of everyone who loved him and I honored a man whose relationship with me was so complex and filled with honor and love.

Standing there, I told his story. The one I saw. The one I knew. My dad was a proud man. Extremely proud. Proud of his family. Proud of his girls. Proud when he walked into a room. Proud of the things he'd accomplished. Proud of his heritage. Proud of his German roots. Proud to be American. Proud to be my dad. And he taught us how to be proud of ourselves. He taught us to comb our hair, wash our faces, be dressed and ready. He'd hand us the comb from his back pocket when we needed it, a silent reminder to go fix ourselves. He taught us to hold our heads up high and not to take grief from anyone about anything.

That pride came from somewhere. He was born and raised dirt poor in Victor, California. His parents, Mary and Russell Meidinger, barely scraped by. He was picked on relentlessly as a boy. And he carried that with him.

One day, my grandfather Russell sent my dad to school in a brand new shirt and new pants. Dad came home with them ripped and torn. He told his father he'd been picked on and beaten up. Russell looked at him and said: "If you come home again with your shirt torn, you'll have to deal with me. Next time that kid picks on you, you ball up your fist, you punch him square in the face, and you don't stop until he's down. And you don't come home until it's done."

The next day, my dad handled that kid. He came home with a perfectly good shirt. And he was proud to tell his father that.

From that moment on, anyone who crossed him, anyone who made him feel inferior, anyone who made him feel small or weak or poor, he would ball up his fist and never back down. That fire. That vengeance against anyone who tried to make him feel less than. It stayed with him his entire life.

And he passed it to me.

My dad and my son Rowdy had a bond I can't fully describe. They spent every week together from the time Rowdy was born. Dad taught him everything. How to make sauerkraut, bratwurst, whiskey, and wine. How to ferment foods. How to grow and preserve fruits and vegetables. How to fix things when they're broken instead of just buying new. He taught him music. Bought him guitars. Encouraged him to play and sing. He sponsored Rowdy's baseball teams and rodeo competitions. Showed up to every event. Stood behind him no matter what.

Rowdy adored him. Learned from him. Became who he is because of him.

And now, Rowdy is taking over the business my dad built from the ground up. With my mother's help, Rowdy will continue the legacy. The sauces, the seasonings, the tradition. That's how you honor someone. You continue what they started.

A couple weeks after he died, I stopped by my parents' house. I was digging around in the fridge and freezer, looking for something to make. And I found a bag of my dad's bratwurst. It was marked with Sharpie. Made in May 2025. It had been in the freezer for months. Everything my dad made was dated, organized, detailed. You always knew exactly when he made something. That was just who he was.

I pulled out that bratwurst. Warmed it up. Got some of his sauerkraut. Put it on my plate.

And I started sobbing.

Because I realized: This was the last meal my dad would ever make for me. His love. His energy. His care, all went into that food. To nourish me. To feed me. That was so important to him. Making sure we were cared for and well fed. And even though he was gone, he was still feeding me. Still taking care of me. One last time.

Standing at his funeral, delivering his eulogy, I said: "I speak today with pride. I speak on his behalf, to honor him as the good, proud family man who secured his heritage and showed the world that he was someone to be proud of."

Thundered roared in the sky behind me. Three times. The only time in the day it happened. He heard me tell the world that I was proud of him. Proud to be his daughter. That was the only thing that mattered to me.

The girl he doubted. That girl stood in front of everyone and honored him.

Because you can honor someone while acknowledging the complexity. You can love someone deeply and still recognize the ways they challenged you. You can be grateful for what they taught you and still grieve that it took so long to hear the words you needed.

My dad taught me to be tough. He taught me to be strong. He taught me to ball up my fist and never back down. He taught me that who you are and where you come from is something to be proud of. He taught me that family is the only thing that matters. And he taught me, through his silence, through his fear, through his eventual pride, that you keep showing up even when it's hard.

I couldn't have done any of this without him. Not the photography. Not the businesses. Not the ranch. Not Ropers Sports News. Not the books. Not the legacy. All of it required the toughness he gave me. The resilience. The refusal to quit. The determination to prove I belonged.

He made me who I am. Even when he didn't believe in what I was doing, he made me strong enough to do it anyway.

I miss him. I miss our talks. His advice. His endless wealth of knowledge about engineering, farming, construction, food, and tradition. I miss sitting on the back porch with him, watching the ranch come alive, hearing him say he was proud of me. I miss the daily phone calls about Ropers Sports News. I miss the man who was always right behind me, even when I couldn't see him, even when he was silent, even when it hurt.

He was there. And now he's not. And some days, the free falling still takes my breath away.

Family comes first. Always. Even when it's hard. Even when it's complicated. Even when the relationships are messy and painful and full of silence. You hold on to every thread you can. Because you never know when it's the last one.

He never quit fighting. He was always fighting. He told me so himself, in that car, on the way to the hospital. The last real words he ever said to me. He heard me that day in the sun, screaming at him to fight. And he wanted me to know that he did. Until the very end.

Thank you, Dad. For making me tough. For making me strong. For teaching me that family is the only thing that matters. For showing up even when you didn't understand. For being proud of me even when it took you years to say it. For the steaks we shared while they were still cooking. For the soup we made when the lights went out. For the logos on your truck. For the daily calls. For the golden seal on Ropers Sports News. For believing in me, completely, with no doubt. And for never quitting. For always fighting. Just like you taught me.

I am proud of what you left behind. I am proud to be your daughter. And I carry you with me always.

* * *

[THE LESSON]: Family First — Hold Every Thread

You can honor someone while acknowledging the complexity. You don't have to sanitize someone's memory to love them. Real love holds space for both the good and the hard.

Someone can challenge you and make you who you are. The toughness you resent might be the gift you need. The hardness, the silence, the disapproval, that might be exactly what saves you later when you survive foreclosure, rebuilding, resistance, skeptics.

Approval delayed is not approval denied. If you keep showing up, keep building, keep proving yourself, keep loving them even when it hurts, they might get there. My father's golden seal on Ropers Sports News, after a lifetime of doubt, was worth the wait.

Family is the only thing that matters. Hold on to every thread. You never know when it's the last conversation. The last meal. The last chance.

Legacy lives in what you pass down. What matters isn't fame or money, but what you teach the next generation. What they carry forward after you're gone.

Grief and gratitude can coexist. Miss them and thank them at the same time. That's what real love looks like.

[YOUR TURN]

First: Who in your life has a complex relationship with you that deserves acknowledgment?

____

____

Second: What thread are you holding on to right now?

Third: What are you passing down?

19

Permission Granted

I was a poor kid from Lockeford, and somehow, through all of that, I built this: A photography career that's spanned decades and documented thousands of women. A book series preserving Western culture. Owner and publisher of a successful women's magazine. Farmer. Real Estate investor. Owner of a 58-year-old legacy publication. A platform teaching others how to build their own empires. A life I didn't inherit. A life I created.

I wrote my own damn story. And if I can do it, you can too. Let me tell you how this book came to be.

In late 2025, I was asked to speak at the Cowgirl Collective in Cartersville, Georgia. When I got that invitation, I was overwhelmed with honor. Because I have so much to say. I enjoy motivating and inspiring people every single day, not only within my relationships, but also in my writing, in my magazines, in my photos. This is what I do. This is who I am.

So when I was asked to speak, I took it extremely seriously.

I had been asked to speak a couple of times before, and I had all of this content that I wanted to share. For the last year, I had files on my computer full of inspirational ideas and pieces of my story. I had been transcribing things constantly on my phone, journaling in my notes app, capturing ideas and thoughts and the things that helped me achieve what I've done. How I've been able to manage it all. How I've kept my mind and my emotions and my life in balance and harmony. The real key points in how I do these things.

So I created a mastery list. A principles list. All of these ideas I'd been collecting, organized into something I could teach.

Then I developed an outline for the talk. It was only supposed to be 30 minutes, so I paired it down into condensed ideas and condensed storylines. I made key points. I got really good at organizing my thoughts.

And that's one of the most important things: organizing your thoughts. Looking at something from A to Z and all the steps in between. How do you get there? What's the path? What are the principles that actually work?

That outline for the talk ended up becoming chapters. It became the bones of a book.

And then I had so much to say that within those bones, I was transcribing information, building out each section based on that outline. I took all of my transcriptions, all of my notes, all of my ideas, and I developed it into the book you're holding right now.

I used technology to help me write it.

AI became my editor. At the end of 2025 and the beginning of 2026, I began implementing AI as a tool in my creative process. And it has become life-changing. Every single day, I'm excited about what this technology can do because it is helping me get all of my ideas and all of my stories down in organized fashion, into chapters, into something that actually makes sense.

Don't let anybody ever downplay the use of technology as tools. It has become one of the most important tools I've ever had. And it's the reason this book is completed today.

I implemented all of my skills in getting this on paper. Starting messy. Getting paint on the canvas. Not being afraid. Using everything I had, every tool available, every principle I've learned over 25 years. That's what mastery looks like. You don't wait for perfect conditions. You use what you have. You start ugly. You refine as you go.

And now this book exists. Write Your Own Damn Story. A companion to the keynotes I'm presenting. A guide for anyone who's been told they can't, who's been silenced, who's been doubted. Proof that the girl who failed English can write a book. That the woman who was told she'd never make money with a camera can build an empire. That you can take your mess and turn it into your message.

Let me tell you something about roadblocks: How you handle them shapes your story. It's not about avoiding obstacles. It's about what you become when you push through them.

Every setback I faced taught me something I couldn't have learned any other way. Losing everything and rebuilding taught me resilience. Bending the knee at HERLIFE taught me never to compromise my voice for a paycheck. My dad's silence taught me to believe in myself even when the people I love most can't. The good old boys' club taught me to stand my ground and prove my worth through work, not words. The bitch club taught me jealousy is wasted energy and abundance is the only mindset worth having.

Every single obstacle became a lesson. Every failure became fuel. Every person who doubted me became proof that I could do it anyway. The pain was the point. Not because I needed to suffer. But because I needed to grow strong enough to carry what I was building.

And you do too.

Looking back at this journey, from the $600 Costco camera to owning The Roping Bible, I can see the patterns now. The strategies that actually worked. The principles that made the difference. Not theory. Not fluff. But real, tested, proven methods for building something that lasts.

Here's what mattered most:

Get paint on the canvas. Stop waiting for perfect. Start ugly.

Refine as you go. The hardest part of any project is starting before you're ready.

Network deep, not wide. Build real relationships with people you respect. Sharon Camarillo opened doors I didn't even know existed, not because I asked, but because I showed up with integrity.

Start where you are with what you have. I didn't wait for the perfect camera or the perfect credentials or the perfect moment. I started with a Costco camera and curiosity.

Family first. Always. Money comes and goes. Success rises and falls. But family is the only thing that actually matters. Hold every thread.

You can't create from competition. When I honored Bob Feist's legacy instead of competing with it, I built something better than I could have built alone.

Emotional mastery is everything. You can't heal in the environment that made you sick. Sometimes you have to remove yourself, ground yourself, and rebuild from a place of wholeness.

Jealousy manifests lag. Abundance manifests opportunity. Be happy for others' success and you create space for your own.

Legacy work is hard. Do it anyway. The road is exhausting. The resistance is real. But 50 years from now, the work will matter more than the comfort.

These aren't just lessons I learned. They're the foundation I built on. And they work.

So where am I now?

I'm raising my son Rowdy, who's taking over his grandfather's business and building his own legacy. I'm living on a ranch in California with my family, growing gardens, preserving food, practicing the old ways, staying grounded.

And I'm stepping into the next chapters of my career: speaking, motivating, writing, and educating.

This is what I'm building now. Not just publications. Not just books. But a way to help others get their work out into the world.

Because here's what I've realized: there are people right now with brilliant ideas, powerful stories, cultures worth preserving, and they don't know how to get it done. They don't know where to start. They don't have someone who's actually done it, who's mastered it, who can show them the path.

I spent over a decade figuring this out. The hard way. Through trial and error. Through expensive mistakes. Through years of building systems that actually work.

And now I want to give that to others.

<u>Publishing Mastery Academy</u> is where all of this comes together. It's the umbrella for everything I'm teaching. Within

it, <u>Magazine Mastery</u> is a course specifically for publishing magazines, but the Academy covers so much more.

Magazine publishing. Book publishing. Photo publishing. Music publishing. Mindset and emotional mastery. Using technology in your business. How to implement your publishing into digital content. Whether you want to create sports programs, business mailers, something simple, or a complex monthly publication. Whether you want a full career in publishing and you want to know how to do it, how to be available and ready, how to build something that lasts.

And here's something I need you to understand about print: it is the essence of permanence.

The internet can be deleted. Blog posts and websites are taken down every day. Social media accounts are removed, suspended, erased. Your digital content can disappear overnight and there's nothing you can do about it. But when something is in print, it is forever. You can't take it back. You can't delete it. It exists as a physical artifact that will outlast servers and algorithms and platform changes.

Print is sustainable. Print is real. Print lasts a lifetime. And print is regarded and respected higher than any other media because of that permanence. When you hand someone a magazine or a book, you're handing them something tangible. Something that will sit on their coffee table, their bookshelf, their desk. Something their grandchildren might find someday. That's legacy. That's what we're building here.

This is a fast-track to independence. To freedom. To building something that's yours.

When you learn how to publish, when you build your own platform, you gain more than a skill. You gain influence. You gain a network. You gain a career that you control. You gain income streams that compound over time. You gain the ability to preserve the stories and cultures you care about. You gain a legacy that will outlast you.

This is what I built for myself. And this is what I want to teach others to build.

If you've ever dreamed of getting your ideas on paper, of creating a magazine or a book, of building a publishing business or even a franchise, this is how you do it. Not in years. Not through expensive trial and error. But through proven systems taught by someone who's actually done it. Someone who's mastered it. Someone who built multiple publications over more than a decade and knows exactly what works.

The people who succeed in publishing aren't necessarily the most talented. They're the ones who get the right guidance. Who learn from someone who's already walked the path. Who skip the mistakes that cost time and money and heartbreak.

That's what Magazine Mastery provides. A roadmap. A mentor. A community. And a fast-track to building your own empire.

Because here's what nobody tells you about legacy work: It

doesn't get easier if you wait. The elders get older. The culture erodes faster. The stories fade. The window closes. I'm racing against time right now with the Western Elders Series. Every month I wait, someone passes away with knowledge that can never be recovered.

That's not meant to scare you. It's meant to wake you up. Your vision has an expiration date. Not because you'll run out of time. But because the stories you want to preserve are disappearing right now, while you're waiting to feel ready.

Here's the thing about writing your own story: You don't need permission.

You don't need credentials from institutions that would have failed you anyway. You don't need approval from people who are too afraid to take risks themselves. You don't need to wait until you feel ready, because you'll never feel ready.

You just need to start.

And here's what I know about you right now: You picked up this book for a reason. Somewhere inside you, there's a story screaming to get out. A vision you've been sitting on. A culture you're terrified will disappear. A legacy project that keeps you awake at night.

Maybe it's a magazine about barrel racing or vintage motorcycles or sustainable ranching. Maybe it's a book documenting your grandmother's recipes or your grandfather's cowboy poetry or the last generation who remembers how things used to be done. Maybe it's something nobody else understands yet, something so specific to your world that you think nobody would care.

But here's what I learned photographing over 1,000 women and documenting Western culture for 25 years: The stories that scare you to tell are the exact stories the world is desperate to hear. The more specific you get, the more universal it becomes.

When I started photographing cowgirls in California, people said the market was too small. Now I own a 58-year-old publication and I'm building a series that will outlive me. The thing you think is "too niche"? That's your goldmine. That's your legacy. That's the thing nobody else can do because nobody else has lived your specific life with your specific access to your specific world.

So let me ask you something: What story dies with you if you don't tell it? What culture disappears if you don't document it? What voices go silent if you don't give them a platform?

That's not a hypothetical question. I want you to actually feel that.

Because right now, as you're reading this, there's someone in your world whose story matters. An elder who remembers the old ways. A craftsperson keeping a dying art alive. A community that's being erased by progress. And if you don't preserve it, if you keep waiting for permission or the perfect time or someone more qualified, that story vanishes. Forever.

Here's my promise to you: If you have a vision for a magazine or book that preserves something you love, I can show you exactly how to bring it to life. Not might. Not maybe. Not "we'll see." I can. Because I've done it. Multiple times. In multiple industries. Through every obstacle you can imagine.

And I'm still here. Still building. Still creating. Still preserving stories that matter.

But here's what I need from you: Stop waiting for permission. It's not coming. Stop waiting to feel ready. You never will. Stop waiting for perfect conditions. They don't exist.

The time is now. The permission you need is already yours. And the person who has to believe in your vision first is you.

In five years, you'll either have brought your vision to life or you'll be explaining why you didn't. You'll either be holding your published magazine in your hands or wishing you'd started. You'll either be documenting the stories that matter or watching them disappear.

There's no neutral position. You're either building your legacy or you're letting it die.

And I know which one you're going to choose. Because you read this entire book. You stayed with me through the failures and the obstacles and the hard lessons. You're still here. That tells me everything I need to know about you.

You're the person who finishes things. The person who does

hard things. The person who's been waiting for someone to say: Your vision matters. Your story deserves to be told. You belong in this work.

So I'm saying it: Your vision matters. Your story deserves to exist. You belong in this work.

And I'm here to help you build it.

This is your invitation. Not to copy my path. But to build your own. With your vision. Your voice. Your story. Your culture. Your legacy.

I'll be here with the frameworks that actually work. The community who gets it. The support when it's hard. The celebration when you succeed. Everything I learned building multiple successful publications so you can skip the painful trial and error and go straight to what works.

Let's build something together that outlasts us both. Let's preserve the stories that matter. Let's document the cultures we love. Let's create magazines and books and legacy projects that will still matter when we're gone. Let's prove that people like us, people who started with nothing, people who were told we'd never make it, we get to write our own stories.

And nobody can stop us.

Now go write yours.

Your next chapter starts right now.

With love and absolute belief in what you're about to create,

Dee Yates

Publisher, Photographer, Author, Speaker, Mentor,
   And a girl from Lockeford who refused to let anyone else write her story.

* * *

Ready to Write Your Own Story?

The Magazine Mastery Course isn't just education. It's a legacy builder. It's the bridge between your vision and reality.

Learn more and join the movement at DeeYates.com

For speaking inquiries, coaching, and mentoring: I'm here. I'm available. And I believe in what you're building.
Your story is waiting. Let's bring it to life together.

* * *

For Rowdy, who will carry the legacy forward.
For my father, who taught me to be tough enough to do it.
Who never quit fighting. Who was always fighting.

For the cowgirls and elders whose stories deserve to be told.

And for you, the person reading this right now whose vision is about to change the world.

This is your time. No more waiting. No more asking for permission. No more excuses.

Permission granted.

www.ingramcontent.com/pod-product-compliance
Lightning Source LLC
Chambersburg PA
CBHW050322160726
48002CB00001B/139